GUIDE TO PHOTO GRAPHY

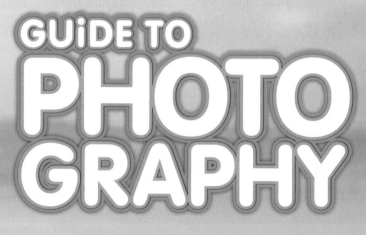

Tips & Tricks on How to Be a Great Photographer From the Pros & Your Pals at

Nancy Honovich

and National Geographic Photographer Annie Griffiths

NATIONAL GEOGRAPHIC
KIDS

WASHINGTON, D.C.

CONTENTS

Foreword by Annie Griffiths — 6

Be a Photographer and Share
Your Shots! — 8

How to Use This Book — 9

Photography Timeline — 10

Getting Started: Annie's Tips — 12

EQUIPMENT BASICS

How a Camera Works — 16

Lens Types — 18

Digital Cameras — 20

Point-and-Shoot Cameras — 24

Smartphones — 26

Annie's Assignment:
Find a Scene and Wait — 28

Underwater Cameras — 30

Video Cameras — 32

Annie's Assignment:
Turning Cute Into Candid — 34

Film Cameras — 36

Toy & Disposable Cameras — 38

Camera Care — 40

HOLD IT RIGHT ... AND FOCUS

The Cure for Blur — 44

What You See Is What You Get — 46

Carrying Tips — 48

Annie's Assignment:
Create a Doorway Studio — 50

Secrets of the Trade: Photo Editing — 52

Fixing and Faking — 54

Color Correction — 56

Annie's Assignment:
Create a Sports Story — 58

What File Should You Use — 60

Storing Your Photos — 62

Showing Off Your Photos — 64

Take the Challenge — 66

Get Crafty — 68

SEEING THROUGH THE LENS

Human Eye vs. Camera Eye — 72

Autofocus Lens — 74

Annie's Assignment: Choosing Your Focus — 76

Depth of Field — 78

Shutter Speed — 80

Capturing Light Quality — 82

Annie's Assignment:
Balancing Twilight With Ambient Light — 84

Quality of Daylight — 86

Lighting Directions — 88

Shadow Play — 90

Annie's Assignment: Long Exposures — 92

Indoor Lighting — 94

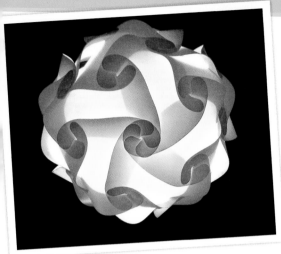

Flash 96
Night Photography 98
 *Annie's Assignment: Turn a Flashlight Into a Photo Paintbrush* 100
Secrets of the Trade: Tricky Lighting Situations 102

YOUR BEST SHOT
Composition 106
The Main Attraction 108
Framing Your Shot 110
Move In for a Closer Shot! 112
Annie's Assignment: Capture the Light in Their Eyes! 114
Backgrounds 116
Off Center: Rule of Thirds 118
Vertical or Horizontal? 120
The Secret to Storytelling 122
Capturing Details 124
Annie's Assignment: Let Patterns Lead Your Composition 126
Point of View 128

MAKE YOUR SUBJECT RULE
Portraying Animals 132
Annie's Assignment: Wildlife in Your Own Backyard 134
Capturing People 136
Capturing Events 138
Annie's Assignment: Photographing a Group 140
Secrets of the Trade: Extreme Weather 142
Shooting Landscapes 144
Capturing Travel 146
Annie's Assignment: Turn Your Vacation Into a Picture Story 148

Equipment Settings 150
Quick Tips 151
Glossary 152
Equipment Basics 154
Resources 155
Index 156
Credits and Acknowledgments 158

ANNiE GRiFFiTHS

WHEN I WAS GROWING UP, very few kids had cameras of their own. Film was expensive, so we would shoot only a few pictures at a time. Kids today are lucky! Digital cameras come in so many sizes and prices that there's a camera for everyone. Nearly five trillion pictures have been taken since photography was invented, most of them in the past ten years!

Although I always loved pictures and pored over magazines such as *National Geographic*, I didn't get my own camera until college. Since then, the camera has become a passport that has taken me to more than 150 countries: I've photographed everything from camels to elephants to ultralights. I've crossed deserts, climbed mountains, and camped in the Arctic. Most important, the camera has taken me into the lives of hundreds of people.

Photography is part skill, part art, and part passion. This book will guide you through all three. It is essential for photographers to understand how their cameras work. Automatic settings are great, but if you want to make artistic choices, you must know how to override those settings—and this book will show you how. You will also learn the basics of composition, light, and capturing moments.

The best way to use this book is as a guide. Feel free to jump around to sections you're curious about. Most sections include an "assignment" I give you to help you practice the techniques you learn. It will also give you ideas about what to do with the pictures you like best.

When you've selected your favorites, be sure to upload them to National Geographic Kids My Shot—we can't wait to see what you create!

LOOK FOR ANNIE'S ASSIGNMENTS

Throughout the book you'll discover sections labeled "Annie's Assignment." Each one gives you the basics of how to shoot a certain topic or situation, ranging from sports to backyard wildlife to travel. Some will focus on a technique, such as tips for getting a good candid shot or capturing fireworks at night. Annie also shares her secrets to making winning photos.

Annie gives you an assignment.

ANNIE'S ASSIGNMENT

TURNING CUTE INTO CANDID

BABIES AND PETS ARE SO CUTE that we sometimes forget that photographers still have to work hard to make great pictures of them. Beautiful light, thoughtful composition, and precious moments will turn a cute picture into a wonderful photograph.

FUN FACT

A YOUNG COWBOY SHOWS OFF HIS "STEER."

Pets are superstars on the Web! According to the Telegraph newspaper in Britain, one in ten pets has a social media pr...

TRY YOUR OWN: CUTE CANDIDS

stopping. Try not to dictate their slumber, but take the opportunity to photograph details while they quietly holding still?

Bring Fido into the shot. If you're photographing people who are shy or stiff, sometimes getting a beloved pet or a sweet child in the picture will loosen things up and encourage natural interactions.

STEPS

Remember that photographs of children and pets are best when we see the world from their point of view, so get on your knees or stoop down to take your pictures.

Accept that you have very little control over animals and babies. You must be patient until they do something naturally. While you are

waiting, think about your composition and exposure so that you are ready when the moment happens.

Focus on their eyes! The eyes are the window to the soul, so look for ways to feature these baby blues in your shot.

Remember that some of the sweetest portraits can happen when an infant or a pet is ...

EXPERT TIP

Photographing kids or animals can be challenging if they are in an active mode. Try to choose times when they are warm, well fed, and slightly tired to make portraits.

34   35

Try Your Own: Annie walks you through the steps.

Expert Tips: Annie or another pro shares a tip for getting the shot you want.

Fun Fact: Annie's surprising fact could be from history or today.

7

BE A PHOTOGRAPHER AND SHARE YOUR SHOTS!

Show us your pet acting funny, a weirdly colored flower, or an oddly shaped shadow that resembles your Aunt Marge!

MY SHOT—AN ONLINE PHOTO COMMUNITY by National Geographic Kids— gives photographers (you!) the opportunity to share your photos with the world. Members upload pictures showing all kinds of subjects. Check them out in this book.

To join, go to the My Shot homepage at ngkidsmyshot.com and click the Sign-up button. All you need is the permission of a parent or guardian and any kind of camera to get started. Then you'll choose a username, so no one knows your actual identity.

"Users are supportive and greet new users with encouragement," says Laura Goertzel (user LauraStar), who oversees the site. "We're like a family."

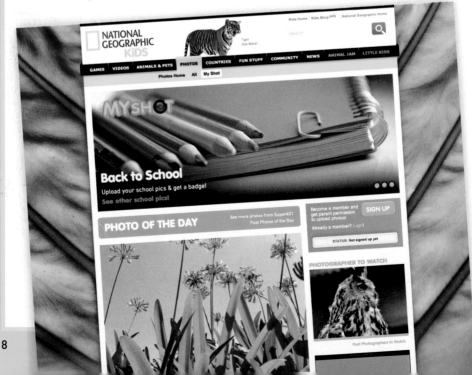

HOW TO USE THIS BOOK

While you're learning to be a photographer, check out the tips and tricks from the pros on every page.

Hot Shot: National Geographic photographers tell you how they got their winning shots.

What Went Wrong?: Based on the information on these pages, try to figure out why a shot's not working.

Did You Know?: Find out the stories behind photos of today and yesterday.

What You Should Know: These bullets give you clear information about equipment and techniques.

Careers for Camera Hounds: There are lots of career options for photo lovers. Meet National Geographic staffers who work with photographs in many different ways, from archiving to studio shooting.

Q&As: Pros tell you why they started photographing or loving pictures and how they got a start—many at their school publications.

Expert Tip: Throughout the book, Annie Griffiths and other Nat Geo photographers share their tips for getting the shot you want.

Technique: Some pages focus entirely on techniques, such as lighting. You'll find photos with captions that tell you what's going on in the picture and how you can do it, too.

PHOTOGRAPHY TIMELINE

TODAY YOU CAN TAKE A PICTURE AND SHARE IT with your friends in the same amount of time it takes you to read this sentence. But that wasn't always the case. Check out the timeline below to see how major discoveries and advances in technology have helped pave the way for photography as we know it today.

5TH CENTURY B.C.E.
Chinese philosopher Mozi notices an interesting phenomenon: When sunlight enters a dark room through a small hole, it projects an upside-down image on the opposite wall.

1558
Italian scientist Giambattista della Porta calls this phenomenon camera obscura, which is Latin for "dark chamber." He encourages artists to trace the projected image so that the objects in their paintings look accurate. Over time, many do—including Dutch painter Johannes Vermeer.

1840
William Henry Harrison becomes the first U.S. president to be photographed while in office. Unfortunately, the photo is lost! So the oldest surviving photo of a U.S. president is a daguerreotype of John Quincy Adams taken after his presidency.

1826
Frenchman Nicéphore Niépce creates the first permanent photograph using camera obscura and a pewter plate coated with asphalt. The image shows the view outside his window.

1853
Photojournalism takes off when a Romanian artist named Carol Szathmari takes photos of the Crimean War. Szathmari lugs his bulky camera equipment to the battlefield in a wagon.

1877
American Eadweard Muybridge develops a fast shutter that helps him take photos of objects in motion. His most famous series of photos shows a galloping horse.

1884–1888

George Eastman, once a New York bank clerk, invents film by coating special paper with dry gel. It replaces chemically treated plates. In 1888, he introduces the easy-to-use Kodak and then the smaller $1 Brownie in 1901.

1907
The autochrome plate is created by the French Lumière brothers, who had produced motion pictures in the late 1800s. The autochrome (below) becomes the first successful color photography and sets the stage for future color innovations.

1920

A German company called Leica introduces a small, portable camera that can take high-quality photos. The camera uses 35-millimeter film, a type of film that had been previously used to make movies.

1937
After Edwin Land takes a photo of his three-year-old daughter, she wants to know why she can't see the result immediately. This inspires Land to create the first instant camera—the Polaroid.

1975

Steven Sasson, an engineer at Eastman Kodak, builds a digital camera. It records black-and-white images on cassette tape and weighs eight pounds. That's heavier than a brick!

1987
An American company called MegaVision begins selling the Tessera, a digital camera designed for use in commercial photo studios. The digital revolution grows!

2014
Sony and other companies release 4K video cameras with ultra-high definition, which capture the high-quality detail of even a tiny hair.

GETTING STARTED
ANNIE'S TIPS

BY ANNIE GRIFFITHS

TAKING A PHOTO IS AS EASY AS PUSHING A BUTTON, but taking a good photo requires patience and a general understanding of how photography works. Whether you're using a low-end smartphone or a high-end digital camera, check out my top tips for taking better pictures. These pointers—and many others—will be discussed in greater detail later in the book, but to get started:

 TIP 1

Get Closer When You Photograph People

Remember, it's the face of a person that makes us love people pictures, not their shoes! So move in close and show that beautiful face!

TIP 2

Take Time to Think About Your Composition

Composition is the way you place objects or people inside the frame. This is where you can be most creative. Remember, what is left OUT of the frame is as important as what is left in, so look carefully to see if anything in the shot will distract from your subject. If so, find a way to recompose, or rearrange, the photo so the distraction is left out.

composition: the arrangement of the subject and its surroundings in a frame

TIP 3
Get Moving!

If you have taken lots of shots from one spot, try looking at the subject from another angle: above, behind, close up, far away. Professional photographers are moving all the time, always trying for a better shot.

TIP 4
Don't Photograph People in the Sun

Bright sun is usually the worst light for photographing people. The sun causes deep shadows and harsh light. Besides, everyone in the picture is usually squinting! It's much better to move your subjects to a shady spot where the light is softer.

TIP 5
Quality Not Quantity

It's far better to take fewer, more thoughtfully composed pictures, than it is to shoot like a maniac. It's not about how many pictures you take. It's about how cool those pictures are!

EQUiPMENT BASiCS

Before you start taking pictures, it's important to know the ins and outs of your camera. On the following pages, we'll take a close look at basic camera features, discuss different cameras, and give you some great tips and tricks on how to use each one.

HOW A CAMERA WORKS

THERE ARE HUNDREDS, if not thousands, of cameras available today—many with unique features. Yet, in spite of these differences, many cameras still share the same basic parts. Here are a few:

Viewfinder

The viewfinder is the small window you look through to see your subject. In some cameras, called single lens reflex (SLR), the light strikes a tilted mirror inside and then is directed upward to a mirrored object called a pentaprism. The image inside the camera is upside down. Once the light bounces off of the pentaprism, it ends up in the viewfinder right side up.

Shutter Button

The shutter button, usually located on the top of the camera, is what you press to take a picture. Pressing this button causes the shutter to open.

Shutter

The shutter is like a small curtain located in front of the sensor or film. When you take a picture, the shutter opens. This allows light to enter and strike the light-capturing system.

Aperture

The aperture is an expandable hole in the lens that controls the amount of light that enters the camera. You can adjust the aperture to let in more—or less—light.

Body

This is the box that supports all the parts of the camera.

Lens

Light rays bounce off the subject and enter the camera through the lens. It focuses the light onto a light-capturing system.

Light-Capturing System

Light rays come together here to form an upside-down image. In digital cameras, a sensor turns light into electronic signals, which the camera turns into an image.

DiD YOU KNOW?

WHEN LIGHT STRIKES THE TOP OF A SUBJECT, it reflects downward into the bottom of the camera lens. Rays that strike the bottom of a subject reflect upward. This creates an upside-down image in the camera. Next, the light hits a mirror, and the image appears right side up in the viewfinder.

MAKE A PINHOLE CAMERA!

In the early days of photography, people relied on pinhole cameras to take pictures. Pinhole cameras use the phenomenon of camera obscura to create images: Light travels through a small hole in a dark box to form a picture. Here's a simple way to make your own pinhole camera and to understand how camera obscura works.

Supply List

- a sharp pencil
- an empty shoe box with a lid
- an X-Acto knife (ask an adult)
- scissors
- a ruler
- wax paper
- tape
- a blanket

STEPS

1. Use a pencil to punch a hole in one of the shorter ends of the shoe box.

2. Ask an adult to use an X-Acto knife to cut a square in the opposite end of the box, directly across from the hole. The square should measure two inches on each side.

3. Use scissors to cut a square of wax paper that measures three inches on each side.

4. Place the wax paper directly over the square you cut in the box. Tape the edges of the wax paper to the box.

5. Take the camera box to a dimly lit room and turn on a lamp. Stand about five feet from the lamp.

6. Cover your head and pinhole camera with a blanket. Be sure that the end with the wax paper is facing you and the end with the pinhole is facing the lamp.

7. Hold your pinhole camera at arms length from your face and aim it at the lamp. Keep it steady until you see an upside-down image of the lamp.

ASK YOURSELF:
How is this similar to the diagram on page 16?

LENS TYPES

THE LENS FOCAL LENGTH—the distance light travels from the lens to the camera sensor—makes a difference in the scene you capture. Telephoto lenses make faraway objects look close; wide-angle lenses capture wide areas in one frame. Follow Annie's tips to choose your lens.

24 mm

Use this wide-angle lens to photograph landscapes. In the foreground, "anchor" your shot with a rock or flower. Viewers feel like they're looking at the scene with you. Or photograph people, but not too closely. They'll look stretched!

35 mm

This is one of my favorite lenses for everyday shooting—a great standard lens. It's a slight wide angle but won't distort people. It's nice for landscapes and active people situations, such as family outings.

55 mm

A 55 mm lens gives a very true rendering of the scene you're shooting—not wide or telephoto. It's excellent for practicing composition and is often used by fine-art photographers. But it won't have the drama of wider or longer lenses.

85 mm

The 85 mm lens is a wonderful portrait lens—a slight telephoto that softens a subject's features. Use it to practice shallow depth of field, keeping only the eyes of the subject in focus, while the background is out of focus.

200 mm

The 200 mm is a medium-length telephoto—for portraits, sports, and wildlife. The longer the lens, the more it compresses features, so it's good for fashion photography. It will make your friends and family look gorgeous!

300 mm

This favorite lens of sports and wildlife photographers is a big telephoto. It's long and heavy, not practical for daily shooting. Photographers graduate to this lens after shooting with smaller lenses for a while.

MAKE A TELESCOPE!

Telephoto lenses, which make a faraway object look close, have focal lengths that are more than 65 mm. Like some telescopes, they use a combination of convex and concave lenses to magnify an object. A concave lens is thinner at the center than at the edge. This spreads out light rays as they travel through the lens. Convex lenses are thicker in the center. This causes light rays to converge, or meet.

For a better idea of how a telephoto lens works, try making a telescope. Here's how:

telephoto lens:
a lens that gives a magnified view of a faraway object

Supply List

- scissors
- 2 paper towel tubes
- masking tape
- a concave lens (take a lens from an old pair of glasses of someone who's near sighted or order one)
- a convex lens (take from a magnifying glass or order one)

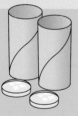

STEPS

1. Use scissors to cut one tube lengthwise, only on one side. Curl one side of the cut edge slightly over the other and tape the top edge down.

❶

2. Insert the cut-and-taped tube into the second paper towel tube. It should fit snugly in the tube but still be able to slide in and out. If not, adjust the size of the inner tube.

3. Tape the concave lens to the end of the inner tube. Tape only around the rim so that you don't cover up too much of the lens. This will be your eyepiece.

❷

4. Tape the convex lens to the end of the outer tube. Again, tape only around the rim so that you don't cover up too much of the lens.

5. Aim your telescope at an object as you look through the eyepiece. You can focus by sliding the inner tube in and out.

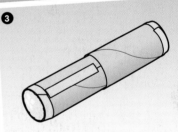
❸

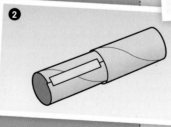

DiGiTAL CAMERAS

The LCD, or liquid crystal display, is the screen that shows the picture. It's made of two glass plates with liquid crystal molecules between them. As light passes through the outer plate, an electrical current aligns the molecules. This allows light to pass through the inner plate to create an image.

DIGITAL CAMERAS TAKE IN LIGHT and convert it into an electronic file that can be uploaded to your computer. When you access this file, you see a picture. Here are some of the digital camera's important features.

Menu Options

When you push the Menu button on the back of the camera, a basic menu pops up on the LCD screen with options such as taking a close-up, using flash, setting a self-timer, avoiding red-eye, or adjusting the ISO to better capture bright situations (100 to 200 ISO) or dark (400 to 1600 ISO). Scroll through the options, then press the OK or Set button for the one you want. Menus vary.

Battery

While a few digital cameras use standard batteries, most come with a rechargeable battery pack developed by the camera's manufacturer. The battery pack is placed into the camera and can be recharged whenever its power is running low.

Memory Card

Digital cameras use memory cards to store photographs. These cards are inserted into a slot in the camera and can be replaced when they're full. The amount of memory a card can store is always shown in a unit of measurement called a gigabyte (see page 60).

64 GB

Zoom Lens

A zoom lens allows you to choose whether to zoom out to take a wider shot or zoom in to take a telephoto picture.

Camera Modes

The mode dial offers manual and automatic settings. Beginners often use the automatic setting and other specialized settings such as landscape and portrait. The main manual setting is M; other manual settings (B, AV, TV, P) allow you to refine automatic settings. (See all settings on page 150.)

Sensor

The sensor is located inside the camera, behind the lens. It's located in the same place that film cameras hold film. The sensor's job is to take the light rays streaming through the lens and turn them into electronic signals. The camera then uses these signals to form a digital image.

OPTICAL IMAGE STABILIZER

6.3mm-31.5mm

1:2.8-4.5

5X OPTICAL ZOOM

POWER

EXPERT TIP

Pick a digital camera that feels good in your hand and that you'll carry with you everywhere. Also, choose a good lens that you can use now—and on your next camera.
—Nevada Wier, photographer

PIXEL POWER

IF YOU LOOK CLOSELY at your computer monitor or television screen, you'll see many tiny dots called pixels. Together, these pixels form a picture. Digital images are also made of pixels.

Resolution is the number of pixels that make up an image. A high-resolution image is one that has many pixels—at least 300 pixels per inch (PPI)—and is therefore very detailed. A low-resolution image—perhaps 72 PPI—has fewer pixels, which results in an image that is "grainy" or less detailed.

high resolution

low resolution

📷 EXPERT TIP

High-resolution images are useful if you like to make prints of your pictures, especially ones large enough to frame and hang on your wall. If you only want to look at your photos online, you may find that photographing in low resolution is best for you. One thing to note: Because high-resolution images require bigger files, they take up much more space on the memory card in your camera and on your computer than low-resolution photos. —Ben Fitch, photo editor

MAKE A PIXEL PORTRAIT!

To get a better idea of how pixels work together to form an image, make a photocopy of this page and follow the steps below.

Supply List

- 4 markers,* 1 in each of the following colors: green, blue, yellow, red

(*If you don't have markers, you can also use crayons or colored pencils.)

STEPS

1. The letter in each square in the grid below stands for a color:

   G=green   B=blue   Y=yellow   R=red

2. Using your markers, fill in each square with the appropriate color.

3. After you've finished, look at the colored grid (page 155). The squares, much like pixels, form an image.

```
G G G G G G G G G G G G G G G G G G G G G G G G G G G G G G
G G G G G G G G G G G G G G G G G G G G G G G G G G G G G G G G
G G G G G G G G G G G G G G G G G G G G G G G G G G G G G G G G
G G G G G G G G Y Y Y Y Y G G G G G G G G G Y Y Y Y G G G G G G G G
G G G G G R R R R R R R Y G G G G G Y R R R R R R R Y G G G G G G
G G G Y R Y Y Y Y R Y R R R R G Y R R Y Y Y Y Y R R R R Y G G G G G
G G G R Y Y Y Y Y Y R Y R R R R R R Y Y Y Y Y Y R Y R B R B G G G
G G R R R Y Y Y Y Y R R R R Y R R R Y R Y Y Y Y Y R Y R R R G G G
G Y R Y Y Y R Y R Y R Y R R R Y R R Y Y R Y R R Y R R B B R G G
G Y R R R Y Y R Y R R R R R R R Y R R Y Y R Y R R Y R R R B G G
G Y R R R R R Y R R Y R R R R R R R Y R R Y R Y Y R R R B G G
G R R R Y R Y R R R R R B R R R R R R Y R Y R R Y R R B R B G G
G Y R R R R R R R R Y R R R B R B R Y R R Y R B R R B R B B G G
G Y R R R R R R R R B R R R R R R R B R B R R R B R R B R B G G
G G Y R Y R Y R R R R R R B R B R R R R R B R B R B B R B R G G
G G R R Y R R R R R B R B R R R R R R R B R B R B R R R B G G G
G G G R R R B R R R R R R R R R B R B R R R R B R R R B B G G G
G G G B R R R B R B R B R R R B R R R R B R B R R R R B B G G G
G G G G R B R R R R R R R B R R R R B B R R R B R R B R B G G G
G G G G B R R R B R B R B R R R B R B B R R B R B R B R B G G G G
G G G G G R B R R R B R B R B R B R R B B R R B R B G G G G G G
G G G G G G B R B R R R B R R R B R R R B B B R B G G G G G G G
G G G G G G G G B R B R B R R R B R B R R R B B G G G G G G G G
G G G G G G G G G R B R B R B B R B B B B B G G G G G G G G G
G G G G G G G G G G B B R B R R R B R B B G G G G G G G G G G G
G G G G G G G G G G G B B R B R R B B R G G G G G G G G G G G G
G G G G G G G G G G G G B B R B B G G G G G G G G G G G G G G G
G G G G G G G G G G G G G G G G G G G G G G G G G G G G G G G
G G G G G G G G G G G G G G G G G G G G G G G G G G G G G G G
G G G G G G G G G G G G G G G G G G G G G G G G G G G G G G G
```

POINT-AND-SHOOT CAMERAS

POINT-AND-SHOOT CAMERAS have fewer features than professional cameras. They're also smaller, lighter, and less expensive. These characteristics make them a popular choice for people who want an affordable camera that can be fully automatic.

WHAT YOU SHOULD KNOW

When it comes to point-and-shoot cameras, it's all in the name: You simply point the camera at a subject and then press the shutter button to shoot. In other words, you don't need a lot of technical knowledge to operate this camera. Still, familiarizing yourself with some of its features can make a big difference:

- The camera's built-in digital zoom lens can be used to get a closer view of a subject that's far away. That may sound great, but the digital zoom often compromises quality by producing pictures that look out of focus. So you may not want to use it too much—or use the optical zoom instead.

- A liquid crystal display (LCD) is a screen located on the back of the camera (see page 20). The LCD allows you to view your images immediately after you've pressed the shutter button. You can also use this feature to view your subject before you take a photo—it presents a more accurate picture than the viewfinder.

- Most point-and-shoot cameras have an automatic flash that goes off in dark and low-lit areas. You can turn it off and manually turn it back on when you need it by selecting force flash. Activate the red-eye reduction button to help prevent glowing eyes.

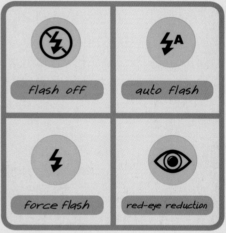

flash off

auto flash

force flash

red-eye reduction

with flash

without flash

EXPERT TIP

It is nearly impossible to view your LCD screen in full sun, so be sure to shade the screen while reviewing the photos you've taken. You can use your own shadow or step into a shady area.
—Annie Griffiths

SMART-PHONES

CELL PHONES HAVE COME A LONG WAY in the past few decades. At first, these devices were heavy and could be used only to make phone calls. But today, you can use your phone for almost anything—sending messages, browsing the Internet, listening to music, and, yes, even taking photos.

WHAT YOU SHOULD KNOW

Many cell phones now have cameras that are as powerful as a point-and-shoot. A phone's sensors, which capture light, are smaller than those in most cameras, but some phones' cameras are still high quality. They also have some cool features.

- **Focus on Filters** If you want to enhance the color of your smartphone photos, there's always an app for that! Many apps have different filters: Sepia-toned filters can add a dramatic effect or vintage feel. Black-and-white filters add drama, too, and if you're new to photography, they can help you pay more attention to the effects of light and shadow in a photo. Color filters can correct colors that are off, and high-contrast filters can make different colors pop.

sepia-toned: the reddish brown color of early photographs from the 19th and 20th centuries

- **HDR Mode** If you notice that the exposure—which gives a subject definition with highlights and shadows—doesn't look as great as it does in real life, there is a solution. Many camera phones now have HDR (high dynamic range) imaging. How does it work? Take a look at the sequence on the opposite page: When you select the HDR option, your camera will take about three photos, each at a different exposure; some will be lighter, while others will be darker. The different photos are then blended together to create one final photo with detail in the light and dark areas. This only works well for still subjects.

EXPERT TIP

Camera phones do best at moderate temperatures. Cold can decrease a phone's battery life, while heat can produce specks on the sensor that make your image look grainy or snowy. In the cold, put the phone in a pocket so body heat keeps it warm. In extreme heat, try to keep your phone in the shade.

—Aimee Baldridge, National Geographic's *The Camera Phone Book*

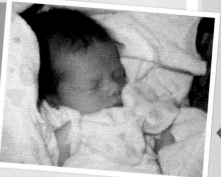

MYSHOT — User: DreamInColour

"I usually photograph in color," says My Shot user DreamInColour, from the UK, but I've seen loads of sepia pics and thought I would have a go myself.

"This flower was an inspiration when I was walking around, looking at things, and trying out new perspectives.

"I intended to have varying focus, but I have a compact camera and can't change the lens on it. Instead, I got up close. I'm pleased with the way it turned out."

HDR IMAGING

Your camera takes photos at different exposures and blends them into a single, evenly exposed image.

too light

combination

too dark

ANNIE'S ASSIGNMENT

FIND A SCENE AND WAIT

STREET PHOTOGRAPHERS ARE FAMOUS for finding a cool scene, choosing a great composition, and then waiting for something wonderful to happen in that scene. It's a terrific way to hone your compositional skills, whatever kind of camera you have.

A STREET SCENE IN COLORFUL ANGANGUEO, MEXICO

📷 EXPERT TIP

Try to choose a scene and a composition in a place where there will be lots of activity. It will give you more chances to capture something candid in your dynamic scene.
—Annie Griffiths

STEPS

1. Look for a striking scene in your neighborhood. It can be a row of colorful houses or a wonderful painted wall or a place where lots of graphic lines meet in a pleasing way.

2. Carefully plan your composition, remembering that what you keep out of the picture is as important as what you keep in. Think of it as a theater set where a scene will play out. Practice shooting as people walk by to see the perfect spot where the figure complements your composition.

3. Then wait ... and wait ... and wait. It may take quite a while, or you may even have to come back to the spot another day. The goal is to get a surprise moment happening in that wonderful scene: a cat curling up in the sunlight or a child chasing a ball or someone jumping over a puddle—a moment of surprise that life creates and you capture.

4. Wonderful street scenes are also great for shooting fashion or environmental portraits. The right scene and composition can set a mood that tells us something about the person or pet or event being photographed.

AN INTERESTING BACKGROUND GETS BETTER WHEN PEOPLE ENTER THE SCENE.

FUN FACT

Perhaps the most famous street photographer was Henri Cartier-Bresson, whose photo at right is an example of his idea of the "decisive moment." That's the instant when a surprising real-life moment happens in a beautifully composed scene.

UNDERWATER CAMERAS

AN UNDERWATER CAMERA is designed with special features that allow the device to work—you guessed it!—underwater. A rubber seal lines the camera's seams to prevent water from getting in, while a thick internal lens is designed to withstand the crushing force of water pressure. Some cameras are water resistant and can also be used in many wet circumstances.

WHAT YOU SHOULD KNOW

The underwater environment can pose many challenges even when you're shooting with a camera that's designed for it. Here's what you should know before you take the plunge:

- It's true that an underwater camera can withstand water pressure—but only up to a certain point. So make sure you know the maximum depth at which your camera can operate.

- Water is a lot denser than air, so you won't be able to get a clear shot of a marine creature, such as fish or coral if you're ten feet away. Try to get close to your subject, and if possible, use a wide-angle lens: It increases the depth of field, which means it will reveal a lot more than can be seen by a human eye looking through a viewfinder.

- Use an internal flash only if you're within three feet of your subject. If you leave it on, you might capture small particles such as sand that are floating in the water.

- Do use a flash if you descend more than six feet below the water surface. At these levels, natural light begins to diminish, so you'll need the extra light from your flash to capture your surroundings.

- If you don't want to invest in an underwater camera, consider using underwater "housing" as an alternative. This is a waterproof container that protects your regular camera and allows you to access the features needed to take pictures.

UNDERWATER CAMERA HOUSING WITH FLASH

PHOTOGRAPHING A LIONFISH

HOT SHOT: David Doubilet

Here I'm photographing a potato cod, a large fish found off a place called the Cod Hole on Australia's Great Barrier Reef. I like to photograph these gentle giants because they are curious and look into the camera. Potato cods on a coral reef tell us that the reef is healthy.

WHAT WENT WRONG?

Use the hints on these pages to figure out why the lighting works in one photo and not the other.

NO

SHALLOW WATER SEA TURTLE WITH A FLASH

YES

EEPWATER REEF
ITHOUT A FLASH

DiD YOU KNOW?

IN 1856, WILLIAM THOMPSON made a splash with the world's first underwater photograph. He took the photo by placing his camera in a waterproof box and lowering it underwater with a pole.

31

ViDEO CAMERAS

VIDEO CAMERAS can capture live-motion video and audio. The first video cameras sold to the public were clunky devices that users had to prop on their shoulders to operate. And if that wasn't bad enough, they recorded footage on videocassette tapes, which often got jammed. Today, video cameras are small—some, like the GoPro, can fit into the palm of your hand. Like digital cameras, they use image sensors to convert light rays into digital signals. This information can then be stored on your computer hard drive, flash drives, or recordable DVDs.

WHAT YOU SHOULD KNOW

Like cameras, different brands and models of video cameras have different features. However, there are a few things common to all:

- **Fully Automatic** All video cameras sold to the public are fully automatic. That means that you don't have to worry about adjusting features such as shutter speed, aperture, and focus—the video camera does it for you! Of course, if you'd like more control, some video cameras do allow you to adjust these settings manually.

- **Flash Memory** You may have noticed the phrase "flash memory" on your computer. It generally refers to the amount of storage space available. Most video cameras have a small amount of built-in flash memory to store your footage. For additional storage, you can purchase flash memory cards.

- **LCD Screen** Much like digital cameras, many video cameras have an LCD screen on which you can view your recorded footage. LCD screens come in different resolutions depending on the video camera. Generally, the higher the resolution, the sharper and more detailed the footage will appear.

📷 EXPERT TIP

When using a video camera, try not to move it ... We have a tendency to whip video cameras around to follow the action (it's called "firehosing" because you look like a fireman waving a firehose back and forth to spread water on a fire). Pick a shot, let it run for ten seconds, and then pick another shot.
—Bob Krist, photographer

MAKE A DOCUMENTARY!

Documentaries are movies that show reality, often by exploring a certain subject. Over the years, documentaries have been made about many subjects, including endangered animals, the fast-food industry, and even spelling bees.

Some filmmakers use video cameras to capture footage for their documentaries—and you can, too!

Supply List

- a pencil or pen
- paper
- a video camera (or video setting on your still camera)
- a computer with an editing program, such as iMovie (Mac) or Windows Movie Maker (PC)

STEPS

1. Think of a subject that you want to explore for your documentary. Some ideas can include:

- Why is my brother such a great video game player?
- Why is my mom—or dad—such a great cook?
- Does my dog think he's human?
- What makes my friends and me so compatible?

2. Create a storyboard. The storyboard is a series of panels (like a comic book) that acts as a blueprint for your movie. It maps out how your documentary will unfold and the order in which any interviews you conduct will appear.

3. Think of a few people you'd like to interview for your documentary and create a shot list. The people you choose should have something to do with the subject of your film. Then write a list of questions you'd like to ask them. The questions should get them to talk about the subject.

4. Begin filming! Start with your interviews. Then shoot footage of anything that will help illustrate the point you are trying to make or what your interviewees have told you. For example, if you're trying to show how your dog thinks he's human, you might film him jumping up in a chair at the dinner table or howling as you sing.

5. Edit your film. When you're done shooting, upload the footage to your computer.

Using a movie-editing program on your computer, drag and drop different scenes in a timeline section so that they appear in the order you prefer. Use your storyboard for guidance, but be open to making changes if you've recorded some great footage that is more interesting than your original story.

6. After you're done, have a viewing party!

ANNIE'S ASSIGNMENT

TURNING CUTE INTO CANDID

BABIES AND PETS ARE SO CUTE that we sometimes forget that photographers still have to work hard to make great pictures of them. Beautiful light, thoughtful composition, and precious moments will turn a cute picture into a wonderful photograph.

A YOUNG COWBOY SHOWS OFF HIS "STEER."

FUN FACT

Pets are superstars on the Web! According to the *Telegraph* newspaper in Britain, one in ten pets has a social media profile!

sleeping. Try not to disturb their slumber, but take the opportunity to photograph details while they are finally holding still!

5. Bring Fido into the shot. If you're photographing people who are shy or stiff, sometimes getting a beloved pet or a small child in the picture will loosen things up and encourage natural interaction.

STEPS

1. Remember that photographs of children and pets are best when we see the world from their point of view, so get on your knees or stoop down to take your pictures.

2. Accept that you have very little control over animals and babies. You must be patient until they do something naturally. While you are

waiting, think about your composition and exposure so that you are ready when the moment happens.

3. Focus on their eyes! The eyes are the window to the soul, so look for ways to feature those baby blues in your shot.

4. Remember that some of the sweetest portraits can happen when an infant or a pet is

 User: Fortheloveofadog

📷 EXPERT TIP

Photographing kids or animals can be challenging if they are in an active mode. Try to choose times when they are warm, well fed, and slightly tired to make portraits. —Annie Griffiths

FiLM CAMERAS

NOT LONG AGO, THE FILM CAMERA ruled the world of photography. Its images filled billboards and magazines and hung on museum walls. But photographers couldn't view, much less delete, a photo after taking it. Also, the images took time to develop. Soon, digital cameras solved these problems. So the film camera became history—or did it? Actually, film cameras are still around, and if you're lucky to have one, you can take great photos with it.

WHAT YOU SHOULD KNOW

● **Film Speed** The ISO (International Organization for Standardization) rating usually ranges from 25 to 3200. The higher the rating, the more light sensitive the film is. So for dim indoor conditions, where your camera needs more light, use a film with a higher ISO, like 1600. Bright conditions call for a lower ISO, like 100. For color or black-and-white film, the ISOs are the same. They are for digital cameras, too (see page 150).

● **Color Film** Color film is made of three layers of dye: red, blue, and green. When the film is being developed, these dyes produce all the colors captured by your camera.

● **Black-and-White Film** Unlike color film, black-and-white film consists of only one layer. When developed, it gives a dramatic look: warmer colors appear dark, while cooler colors appear light.

● **Loading Film** Check the instructions: Some cameras automatically load and rewind film. For manual loading, place the film roll into the camera cradle, then pull the part of the film that's sticking out across the back of the camera until it fits snugly onto the raised sprockets.

● **Developing Film** A photo store can develop your film. First, negative images are made. That means objects that are light in reality appear dark on the film; dark objects appear light. During printing, light shines through the negative onto photographic paper creating a positive image, in which the colors are correct.

MAKE A SUNPRINT!

Developing film requires chemicals to expose an image, but you can make an exposure a simpler way: by using sunprint paper and water. Try capturing cool shapes and patterns on sunpaper by putting it under the sun and then into water.

Supply List

- sunprint paper (from a local craft store or online)
- cardboard
- cool objects to print, such as a peacock feather, a leaf, or a flower petal; they should be flattish
- acrylic sheet (enough to cover the sunprint paper)
- a tub full of water
- lemon juice (optional)

STEPS

1. In a dark place, put a piece of sunprint paper, blue side up, on a sheet of cardboard. (Blue molecules in the paper are sensitive to ultraviolet light, and your images can be exposed quickly, even from sun through a window.) Arrange your objects on top of the paper.

2. Place the acrylic sheet completely and firmly on top of the objects to flatten and hold them to the sunprint paper. This keeps any light from leaking in around the edges.

3. Take your sunprint outside and place it in direct sunlight for two to five minutes. The sun's light stimulates the blue molecules in the paper to take on the forms of the objects.

4. Remove the acrylic sheet and the objects, and then rinse the sunprint paper in a tub of water for one minute. The water causes a reaction that turns the paper's colorless compound into deep blue.

5. To get the deepest blue possible, leave the paper in the water for up to five minutes—or add a little lemon juice to the tub.

6. Put your sunprint on a flat, absorbent surface—a paper towel or a piece of cardboard—to dry.

TOY & DISPOSABLE CAMERAS

IF YOU'RE NEW TO PHOTOGRAPHY, or if you just feel intimidated by the features of a high-tech camera, you might want to start out with a toy or disposable camera. These cameras are easy to use and convenient to replace if they become damaged. This also makes them an ideal choice for outdoor adventures.

TOY CAMERA

Toy cameras are plastic cameras that have been around since the 1960s. Some early models, such as the Diana, had a built-in flash and a few light settings. However, most contained very few features.

WHAT YOU SHOULD KNOW

While things are always changing, one of the most popular toy cameras is still the Holga, composed of a plastic body and lens. Its parts are low quality, so they produce effects that might surprise first-time users. Also:

THE CENTER OF A HOLGA PHOTO IS SHARP; THE EDGES ARE SOFTER.

- The camera's plastic lens is sharp in the center, but softer toward the edges. This will create a soft-focus effect along the edges of your photo.

- The image you see in the camera's viewfinder is slightly higher than what the lens sees, so raise your camera slightly as you take a picture.

- With an older Holga, you'll probably see light streaks in your images. These are light leaks, caused by the film not rolling tightly as you photograph. As you take the film out of the camera, light leaks past the light-tight paper at the edges of the roll. Try folding up a couple pieces of cardboard from the film box and stuffing them under the takeup spool so the film winds tighter on the roll.

HOT SHOT:
Dan Westergren

At Trinidad's annual carnival, I saw this girl in her fantastically bright dress. The vignetting, or fading, of light and focus you get with a Holga's less-than-perfect lens added charm to romanticize the event.

DISPOSABLE CAMERA

Disposable cameras are box cameras usually made of cardboard and plastic. Film cameras have a roll of film that can be processed at a photo lab; then the camera is thrown away. Digital cameras can be reused once the images are uploaded or deleted.

WHAT YOU SHOULD KNOW

Despite being inexpensive, disposable cameras can produce decent photos. Some models are waterproof, making it possible to take underwater shots. Others are panoramic and can produce images that are almost three times longer than they are wide. No matter what type of disposable camera you have, here's what you'll need to know:

- Like the Holga, disposable cameras have plastic lenses that are sharp in the center, but softer near the edges.

- Know the camera's ISO—either its film speed or its sensitivity to light if it's digital—before you buy it. The ISO is noted on the box. Most disposable cameras have film speeds or light sensitivity that range from ISO 400 to ISO 800. Use lower speeds in bright, sunny places and higher speeds in darker indoor areas (see page 150 for more about ISO).

DISPOSABLE UNDERWATER CAMERA

39

CAMERA CARE

LEARNING HOW TO USE YOUR CAMERA is obviously key to taking good pictures, but it won't mean much if you don't take good care of your gear. Check out these tips that Annie finds helpful in the field.

good

bad

Bag It

Camera equipment is delicate, so look for a bag that has strong seams and is made from tough, water-resistant material, such as nylon. The bag should also be well padded, and if possible, have foam dividers that will allow you to keep each piece of equipment separate.

On the Fly

Take air travel into consideration. Checked bags tend to get tossed around a lot, so if you're planning to travel with your camera, make sure the bag is small enough to qualify as carry-on luggage.

Clean Your Lens

Chances are at some point you'll get fingerprints, dust, or water droplets on your lens. If this happens, use a lens pen, lens wipe, a blower (left), or a drop of rubbing alcohol and a soft cloth to gently remove the dirt or smudge. Don't use tissue, which could leave more lint behind and also scratch the lens.

... And Put a Lid on It (a Lens Hood, Too)

To avoid scratches, get a simple UV filter for each lens to protect its delicate coating. Keep your lens cap on when not using your camera. If you have a point-and-shoot camera, your shutter should automatically close over the lens after you've taken a photo. Otherwise, turn your camera off. If you have an SLR camera, place a lens cap over the lens when not shooting. While shooting, protect it with a lens hood, which fits like a collar over the end of the lens and shades from sun glare, too.

Condensation

If you or someone you know wears glasses, you've probably noticed that the lenses fog up when you enter a warm room after you spend time outdoors in icy weather. The same is true when you leave an air-conditioned room and go out in warm, humid weather. This is condensation—and it can happen to your camera lens and body as well. So, before moving from a cold environment to a warm one, or vice versa, place your camera in a plastic bag. Then wait until your equipment has warmed or cooled before using it.

Water Is Your Enemy

Water can damage electronic equipment. (That means your camera!) Saltwater in particular can corrode your gear. So be cautious if it's raining or you're at the beach and risk getting splashed. Some companies sell waterproof camera containers for this purpose, but if you can't splurge, try wrapping your camera in a clear plastic bag and cutting out a hole for the front lens. If you take your camera to the beach, be sure to clean off any sand and salt when you've finished shooting. The best method is to use a cotton swab with a dab of rubbing alcohol on it.

📷 EXPERT TIP

Pssst! Let's be real. If you're outdoors when your camera gets smudged, you may not have the recommended cleaning equipment with you. In this case, just use your breath to fog up the lens and then wipe it off with a cotton T-shirt. —Annie Griffiths

HOLD iT RiGHT ... AND FOCUS!

Knowing how your camera works is important for taking good photos; but you need to know how to hold your camera correctly, too. Making sure your subject is in focus is also key. Whether you're looking at a subject through the viewfinder, sorting your images, or correcting a photo with editing software, it's a visual experience. On these pages find out how to get the best photo, enjoy it, and share it.

THE CURE
FOR BLUR

DO YOUR PHOTOS OFTEN COME OUT BLURRY? Aside from errors in focusing, which we'll get into later, the culprit could be that your body is shaking. Human body tremors are normal and generally nothing to worry about, but they can interfere with your ability to get a good picture. So what can you do to minimize shaking? Knowing the right way to hold your camera is key.

Get a Grip

To reduce body tremors, get a firm grip on your camera. Put your left hand under the camera body to cradle it, and use the fingers of your left hand to hold the lens. Then grasp the side of the camera with your right hand. Use these positions whether you're holding your camera vertically or horizontally.

Elbows in, Feet Apart!

If your hands are in the right position but you're still experiencing camera shake, look at your elbows. Are they sticking out? If so, tuck them in! You'll find that keeping your elbows close to your side or chest, and standing with your feet slightly apart, will help stabilize your body—and your camera.

Wrong

right

The Click of a Button

You might be surprised by how challenging pressing a shutter button can be. If you press too lightly nothing will happen. On the other hand, if you jab the button you might jar your camera and end up with a blurry image. What's the solution? Relax—and with manual focus, press the button using smooth, even pressure. With automatic focus, press the button halfway down to lock the focus and then follow through, pushing down completely to get the shot.

Image Stabilizer

Your camera may have a helpful feature called optical image stabilization. If so, keep it enabled. If your hands are shaking, the camera lens or sensor detects the vibrations and then counters the movement. The result is a much sharper image.

📷 EXPERT TIP

When you don't have a tripod, you can use any stable surface to help you hold still: a rock, a tree, or a backpack. Just be sure to press your camera firmly against the stable surface and depress your shutter carefully.
—Annie Griffiths

WHAT YOU SEE IS WHAT YOU GET

WHEN YOU'RE TAKING A PHOTO, it's important to slow down and compose. Figure out how you want to view your subject and make sure there's nothing unwanted in the frame. You'd be surprised by the number of people who don't do this. Check out some issues that result from this problem below. Are you guilty of any of them?

The Viewfinder

As you look through the viewfinder, or window, of your camera, you'll see a pretty accurate representation of where your subject will be positioned in the photo. You'll also see how much background you'll capture. So pay attention to the edges of the viewfinder window to make sure you're not cropping out any details you'd want to capture.

Straight Shooter

If your picture looks a little lopsided, you probably aren't holding your camera straight. Before you shoot, check to see if your horizon is lined up with the focus point in the viewfinder. This is usually a small rectangle or a series of spots. If it isn't aligned, you'll need to adjust your camera. In addition to a focus point, some cameras have grid lines, which can also help.

EXPERT TIP

After digital cameras first hit the market, many people relied heavily on the cameras' exciting new feature: the LCD screen. After snapping each photo, they would look down at the display to review the image they captured. Everyone around them would do the same and often express their delight by shouting "oohs" and "aahs"—much like a group of chimpanzees. As a result, this act became known as "chimping." And aside from looking foolish, here's why you should avoid doing this too often:

1. You could be missing out on a great photo because you're too busy paying attention to your LCD screen.

2. The more time you spend looking at your LCD screen, the faster you drain your camera battery.

3. You may delete a great photo. The image on the LCD screen isn't always an accurate depiction of what your photo looks like. So, hold on to your images until you've uploaded them to your computer for a better look.
   —Annie Griffiths

Keep Your Eye on the Prize!

When taking a picture, use your "shooter's eye." That's the one that best helps you distinguish depth of field as you look through the lens at your subject. Some shooters feel that keeping both eyes open helps their depth perception—even though only one can peer through the viewfinder.

CARRYING TiPS

PHOTOGRAPHERS LIKE TO CARRY THEIR CAMERAS around as often as possible. That way, if something fun or unusual happens they can record it. This is easy if you're using a smartphone, which is light and can easily slip into your back pocket. But it can be a challenge if you're carrying something more substantial, even a point-and-shoot camera. If this applies to you, here's what you should consider:

Take a Stand: Tripods

Do you enjoy bird watching? Or observing the neighbor's dog as it chases squirrels? Animals make terrific subjects, but they are unpredictable, so it may take some time for you to get a picture. And if you have a heavy camera with a large lens it can feel like forever. If this is the case, you can use the kitchen or picnic table—or consider getting a tripod for support. A tripod is a three-legged stand designed to hold up a heavy camera—so that you don't have to. You can find affordable mini-tripods, including a flexible one that can attach to a fence or pole!

Lighten Up

For your digital camera, it may be tempting to tote all of your different lenses around. But after a while, all that equipment can weigh you down. Instead, think about what you might want to shoot and where. Then pick one lens that's appropriate for the task.

Camera Straps

Camera bags are a great solution when you're going on a long trek. But they're not so practical when you want to snap a spur-of-the-moment picture. For easy access—and camera protection—tote your camera on a camera strap. Make sure that the fabric is strong enough to support your camera and sits comfortably on your body.

MAKE A CAMERA STRAP!

Ease the load of a camera while showing off your personal pizzazz with this stylish camera strap.

Supply List

- 2 large jump rings or swivel hooks* that will fit through the side hooks of your camera
- a small- or medium-size belt, depending on your height (be creative!—buy a colorful new one or use a parent's old belt for a retro look)
- a hammer and a nail
- pliers

(*These can be found online or in your local craft store.)

STEPS

1. Loop one jump ring through the buckle of the belt.

2. Get an adult to help you create a hole in the opposite end of the belt by placing the belt tip over a wooden block and hammering the nail into it.

3. Loop the other jump ring through the new hole.

4. Now use the pliers to put the jump rings through the camera hooks.

5. Close the rings tightly with the pliers and double check to make sure they are secure.

6. For extra security, you can ask an adult to help you solder the metal hoops to the camera hooks—but only if you're not planning to change straps with your look or the season!

EXPERT TIP

An easy-to-carry zoom lens is the 24 to 70 mm. It goes from slightly wide to a nice telephoto. I like it because it allows me to photograph both people and action, and encourages me to get close to my subjects, rather than photograph from far away. —Annie Griffiths

ANNIE'S ASSIGNMENT

CREATE A DOORWAY STUDIO

WHILE YOU'RE ON LOCATION, you can always think of how to improvise to get your best shot. Nobody likes to be photographed in bright sun, which is harsh and unflattering. A shady area just beyond the sun can provide the same soft light that studio photographers use. Find a doorway just out of the sun that has open shade in front, and you can create a studio portrait!

A MUSLIM MAN IN THE DOORWAY
OF HIS HOME IN GALILEE, ISRAEL

📷 EXPERT TIP

This technique can also be used with window light. The key is to expose for the highlighted part of the face and let the rest of the scene be underexposed.
—Annie Griffiths

STEPS

1. On a bright sunny day, find a location where there is open shade in front of a doorway. Open the door and turn off all interior lights so that the background is as dark as possible.

2. Have your model sit outside with the door frame to his or her back.

3. Using a telephoto lens (any focal length will work), compose the image so that none of the doorway shows. The light will be beautiful on the subject's face, and the background inside the doorway will be so much darker than the foreground that it turns to black. Set your aperture (see pages 16 and 78) fairly wide open because you don't need a lot of depth of field for most portraits. Then focus on the eyes. Note: If you are using a long, heavy telephoto, you may wish to use a tripod.

exposure:
the amount of light coming into the camera and the length of time it strikes the digital medium or film. If you overexpose, you've allowed too much light to come in. If you underexpose, you haven't let in enough.

4. Remember to **expose** for the light on the face. Your camera meter will tend to see the dark background and **overexpose**—putting too much light on your subject. So you must usually set your camera to **underexpose** by about one stop (see page 79). Shoot different exposures (see pages 80–81 about exposure and aperture) to see which one is most flattering to the subject's skin tone. The final photos will have beautiful soft light on your model against a completely dark background.

MYSHOT User: ByFaith

FUN FACT

Did you know that fashion photographers often shoot models with very long telephoto lenses? A telephoto, or long lens, compresses features, which makes them appear natural and in proportion without the distortion that can be caused by using a wide-angle lens close to someone's face. A long lens will make any face look lovelier.

SECRETS
OF THE TRADE

PHOTO EDITING

PHOTO EDITING IS AN ART that involves storytelling. It requires going through all the photos you have taken and picking out the great ones from the not-so-great ones to tell a visual story for books, magazines, websites, or advertisements. No one knows that better than **Lori Epstein** and **Kelley Miller**. Lori and Kelley are photo editors for National Geographic Kids. Each day they go through hundreds of pictures to find the few that are worthy of being published. So how do they do it? And how can you do the same? Lori and Kelley share their secrets:

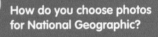

Q1 How do you choose photos for National Geographic?

LE: We think about what our audience would like. Kids generally love colors, so we look for colorful pictures with a lot of contrast.

KM: We also look for pictures that are engaging, or interesting. For example, when we're picking out images of animals, we look for action shots or photos that show an animal looking happy. Kids don't want to see sad animals!

Q2 But I took 200 photos—and they're all great. Are you saying I can't share them all?

KM: Good grief! Don't ever share 200 photos. You might think they're all great, but no one else will, especially if they show the same thing over and over again. Instead, try to whittle it down to 10 to 25 if you want to tell a story.

Q3 That's great. But what if I don't have animals in my pictures? How do I pick out the best ones?

LE: You still need to think of your audience. Let's say you want to send a few vacation photos to your grandmother. She'd be happy with images of you playing in the sand or just having a good time with your family. However, those same images wouldn't cut it with your friends. They'd be more interested in that exciting photo you took of a shark coming out of the water.

grandma friendly

not grandma friendly

Q4 How can my photos tell a story?

KM: Easy. Suppose you're at a birthday party. Try to show the day as it unfolds. That could involve guests arriving at the party, the birthday kid blowing out candles, and then the opening of gifts. It's more interesting to the people who view your pictures. And it'll be more meaningful to you as well because it'll help you remember that moment when you look at them.

📷 EXPERT TIP

Photographers are notoriously bad at editing their own pictures. My advice is:

1. Separate out any pictures that are technically flawed: poor exposures, unintended focus problems, etc.

2. Choose only your best three images from any given subject.

3. Have someone who knows a bit about photography help you choose the very best frame from each situation. Try to separate your memories of the shoot from your choices. Even an adorable puppy must hit the editing floor if it's not one of your stronger images.
—Annie Griffiths

Q5 What about group shots of my friends?

LE: You can still do that, but mix it up a bit. Include a combination of wide shots, where you see a lot of people, medium shots, where you see two or three people, and close shots, where you zoom in on that one person with a giant mouthful of cake. Also, steer away from too many posed photos. People look more interesting when they're being themselves—in other words talking and laughing.

FiXiNG
AND FAKiNG

HAVE YOU EVER CAPTURED AN INTERESTING MOMENT with your camera only to realize the colors in the image are washed out or the subject is not in focus? Fortunately, you may still be able to save the image. Besides editing your best photos to tell a story, there's another, more technical kind of editing you can do: correcting the photo itself. You can do this with editing software. Years ago color correcting a photo was difficult and took hours of work. But today photo-editing software and smartphone apps have made the process faster and easier. So, how can you use these tools to fix some common problems? Read on to find out.

ROTATING, CROPPING, AND SHARPENING

The person or object in your photo appears crooked.

Solution: Editing software can help you straighten your photo or even completely rotate, or turn, it so it's right side up. Simply click the Rotate button to turn the photo until it's in the right position.

rotate:
to turn something, such as a photograph

📷 EXPERT TIP

Always make a copy of the original TIFF or JPEG file and work on the duplicate, saving the original. Keep the file size the same so you won't lose quality. —Kelley Miller, photo editor

Too much background scenery is taking attention away from the subject of your photo.

Solution: You can use the **crop** tool to trim away anything from the image that doesn't belong. To do this, click the Crop button in the tool bar and then use your mouse or trackpad to click and drag a rectangle around the portion of the image you wish to keep. Then hit Return to remove everything outside of the rectangle.

An object you want to call attention to looks slightly blurry.

Solution: You can use the sharpen tool to give an object the appearance of being less blurry. The tool works by playing up the contrast of colors, which fools the eye into thinking a slightly blurry area is sharper than it is. However, it won't fix a photo that is simply out of focus. Use this tool sparingly or your photo will look grainy.

sharpen:
to make an image
appear more detailed

The overall picture appears either too light or too dark.

Solution: You can easily lighten or darken the photo with brightness control. This feature is often found in the Image Adjustments section of the editing software's menu. Simply move the brightness slider to the left to make the photo darker or to the right to lighten it. You can also find the contrast tool in this section. By moving the **contrast** slider you can either increase or decrease the contrast between the light and dark areas of the photo.

contrast:
the degree of difference
between the highlights and
shadows in a photograph

COLOR CORRECTION

Your kid brother forgot to brush his teeth and his smile looks yellow.

Solution: If you wish to lighten only a small part of your photo—like someone's face or teeth—you can use the dodge and burn tools. When you "dodge" an object you make it lighter, and when you "burn" an object you make it darker and less distracting. In this case, you'd dodge the teeth.

yellow teeth

white teeth

Your color photo looks dull.

Solution: You can make a photo more colorful with the **color saturation** tool. Color saturation is usually controlled with a slider. By moving the slider to the left or to the right you can either add or subtract color from your photo. Other tools such as **hue and tint** can also help improve color. But one warning: Use these tools sparingly or your colors will start to look unnatural. The last thing you want is to have your golden retriever look bright orange.

color saturation:
the intensity of a color; the lower the saturation, the paler the colors appear

hue and tint:
the shade and variety of color

CAREERS FOR CAMERA HOUNDS

WHO: Neal Edwards **JOB:** Digital Imaging Technician

Q What does a digital imaging technician do?

A Generally, I use photo-editing software, such as Photoshop, to correct or enhance photos that will be published. That can involve many things. Sometimes, I'll sharpen objects in photos, enhance shadows to make a subject stand out, or I may crop photos to get rid of unwanted elements. I may also have to adjust the colors depending on the readers of the book.

Q How do a book's readers play a role?

A When I'm working on books for adults, the colors are a bit muted. But kids are different. They like really bright colors, so I'll make the colors more vivid.

Q Do you ever do anything unusual to a photo?

A All the time! Recently, while working on a medieval book for kids, I was asked to add an Elizabethan collar to a giraffe's neck!

Q What advice do you have for kids who are interested in this job?

A I'm self-taught, so I learned this job by practicing on my own—and you can, too. If you have photo-editing software, play around with it. Press every button until you know how it works. Also, there is a lot of helpful information online, so mine the Internet for tips.

Your self-portrait looks great except for the bright-red lipstick print Aunt Aurora left on your face.

Solution: Most photo-editing programs have a **clone** tool that allows you to duplicate colors from a good area of your photo and use them to paint over some not-so-good areas. In this case, you'd pick up the colors of your skin and use them to cover up the lipstick print. This tool is also great for removing scratch marks on objects and red eyes that result from using too much flash.

clone:
to duplicate or make an identical copy of something

EXPERT TIP

If colors in your photos seem off, use the color-correcting tool in Photoshop or Photoshop Elements. Find the adjustment tools for color and lightness (sometimes called "curves" or "levels"). Look for three eyedroppers. Experiment with the middle one (gray) and click on something in the picture that should be neutral gray—like someone's gray hoodie. Suddenly the color looks correct.

—Dan Westergren, photo editor

ANNIE'S ASSIGNMENT

CREATE A SPORTS STORY

PICTURES, LIKE WORDS, CAN BE PUT TOGETHER to tell a story. Photo stories need to have a variety of points of view: scene-setting shots, details, and compelling moments. Sports stories are a fun way to start because there is so much action in addition to the actual game—and unless you interfere with play, nobody notices you!

LIFEGUARDS COMPETE IN BOAT
RACES IN SYDNEY, AUSTRALIA.

MYSHOT   User: mckadenator

FUN FACT

Sports Illustrated magazine struggled for years until a visionary editor began adding lots of full-color photographs of the week's sporting events.

STEPS

1. Find a sporting event where you will be allowed to get close to the action. Little league or kids soccer games are easier than trying to get into a college or professional game. Talk with the coach in advance and ask for permission to move around. Promise not to interfere with the game and be mindful as you are shooting.

2. Remember, you will be shooting much more than the game itself. Get there early. Arrive when the team does, or see if you can travel with them on the team bus. Talk to the players about team traditions or superstitions so that you are ready to shoot when those moments happen.

3. Move! Some of the best pictures may be in the dugout or with the fans or from the top of the bleachers. Watch for emotional moments: when the team is losing or winning or the coach is animated. Look for details: shoes, equipment, hands, the mascot.

4. Stay after the game. Great moments often happen after a game is over and the players are either celebrating or licking their wounds.

📷 EXPERT TIP

Sports photography relies on a variety of lenses. Auto-focus helps a great deal when shooting with long telephoto lenses, but you will still want to practice so that you know how fast your shutter speed must be to freeze action.
—Annie Griffiths

MYSHOT User: TheGuyWithACamera

59

WHAT FILE SHOULD YOU USE

DIGITAL PHOTOS ARE USUALLY SAVED in one of three formats: JPEG, TIFF, or raw. What's the difference? Let's take a closer look.

JPEG

JPEG (often shortened to JPG), which is named after its inventors, Joint Photographic Experts Group, is probably the most popular file format for digital photographs. Why? Every computer and digital camera can read this format, so you don't have to worry about not being able to open the file once it's been uploaded to your computer. In addition, JPEGs are smaller than most other file sizes, so they're easy to email and can be stored on your computer without taking up too much space.

DiD YOU KNOW?

A BIT ON BYTES: When you're saving your digital photos, it's important to know how much space they'll take up on your hard drive. Image files are measured in units called bytes. The smallest unit is a kilobyte (KB) and the largest is a terabyte (TB). Here's how the different units stack up.

1,000 kilobytes = **1 megabyte (MB)**

1,000 megabytes = **1 gigabyte (GB)**

1,000 gigabytes = **1 terabyte (TB)**

TIFF

If you're concerned about quality but don't have software that can recognize the raw format, you can save the file as a TIFF (Tagged Image File Format). TIFFs are recognized by most computers. Unfortunately, they are very large and take up a lot of space on your camera, chip, or hard drive. For example, a memory chip that can hold 1,000 normal JPEGs would hold only 70 TIFFs!

HIGH-QUALITY DISPLAY

Raw

No, we're not talking about uncooked food, but we are talking about "uncooked" images. Huh? When you save an image as a JPEG, you remove some data from the file. That's why JPEG file sizes are small. Raw images are different. They are pure, untouched images that your camera has captured—photographers use them for color correcting. Unfortunately, raw files are large and not every computer can recognize the format. As a result, you may have trouble emailing these images to friends.

EXPERT TIP

When you're color correcting a photo, bigger is always better, so opt for a raw or TIFF file. Unlike JPEGs, these large images have plenty of detail and can hold up well to the editing process.

—Neal Edwards, digital imaging technician

STORING YOUR PHOTOS

STORING YOUR PHOTOS IS AN IMPORTANT part of the photography process. It not only creates more space on your camera, but it also ensures that you'll still have your pictures if you lose your camera or accidentally drop it in a pool. After all, cameras can be replaced, but photos cannot.

▶ STORAGE SPACES

Deciding where to store your photos may depend largely on how much space you have on your computer hard drive, or how accessible you want your images to be. Here's the lowdown:

Computer

The obvious place to store your digital photos is on your computer hard drive. Some devices will allow you to do this wirelessly. Otherwise, use a cable that connects directly from your camera or smartphone to the USB port of your computer. If using a camera phone, you'll need to sync your phone to the computer to complete this process.

The Cloud

Smartphones and some digital cameras have Wi-Fi capabilities. If this is true of your camera, consider getting a cloud storage account; your photos will automatically be backed up to a remote storage system, which you can access from every device that's wirelessly linked to the account.

External Drives

Always back up your photos on an external hard drive. It's important for storing your photos, too, since photo files can take up a lot of space on your computer's hard drive. You can also use a smaller, thumb-size flash drive (left), but its storage capacity is much smaller.

THE LIBRARY OF CONGRESS in Washington, D.C., is a research library where many historical documents are stored. The library has more than 13 million photographs in its collection. And you thought you had a lot of photos!

▶ GET ORGANIZED

After you transfer your digital images to your computer, you'll notice that they've been assigned file names something like this: IMG_91848.jpg. This can be challenging when you need to search for a specific photo. To solve this problem, rename each photo file by the date, keeping the serial number, and adding a word before it as an identifier, like: MomsbirthdayMB_91848.jpg. Be sure to keep the extension (.jpg) or your computer may have trouble opening the file. Place the files in folders labeled with the subject names and dates.

▶ GOOD OLD-FASHIONED PRINTS

Technology has changed so much in the past five years (some computers no longer have an optical drive for CDs and DVDs!) that methods we use today to store photos will likely change in the future. To safeguard your photos, try making prints. Many online photo labs can turn your digital images into prints quickly and at a low cost. Then take care of your prints by keeping them in a cool, dry, dust-free environment.

📷 EXPERT TIP

Try a photo organizer tool or "photo library" such as iPhoto. It organizes your photos by date or event when you import them. Some feature facial recognition, which automatically tags images of people you photograph often. They can also pinpoint map locations of photos taken with a GPS-enabled camera. —My Shot team

SHOWING OFF YOUR PHOTOS

AFTER TAKING MANY PHOTOS, you may be left wondering, What should I do with them? While some people enjoy simply having their images stored on their computer or phone for reference, others take it a step further. They share their photos, make prints and frame them, or use them for arts and crafts.

Social Media

Thanks to safe social media communities such as National Geographic Kids My Shot, sharing your photos with family and friends has never been easier. All it takes is creating an account and then uploading your photos. Often, you can write a caption and even tag people and objects depicted in the photo with a hashtag.

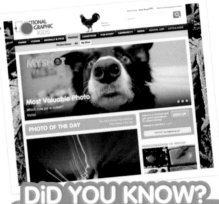

Internet Safety

When you're sharing photos online, pay attention to the privacy settings. Most sites will allow you to choose who sees your photos. This can help you limit access to your friends and family—and keep strangers away. Otherwise, never provide any personal information about yourself online. That means creating a username that doesn't reveal your identity to the public and not geotagging your photo, which would reveal the location of your photo.

Blog About It

When you look at your photos, do you find that many of them show the same subject? Maybe it's food, fashion, places you've visited, your pet, or family. If so, you might want to start a blog about them. To do this, ask an adult to help you choose and set up an account on a kid-friendly site that will host a blog. Then follow the instructions and start blogging!

DID YOU KNOW?

CHANCES ARE, YOU'VE TAKEN at least one selfie in your life. Selfies are portraits that people take of themselves. The word "selfie" is so popular that it was named the Word of the Year by Oxford Dictionaries in 2013. But the word isn't just limited to the English language. Here are a few translations from around the world:

Autoportrait/égoportrait (French)

Egobild (Swedish)

Svayam chitre (Hindi)

Umfanekiso warn (Xhosa, a South African language)

Selbsportrait (German)

Autorretrato/postureo (Spanish)

📷 MAKE A SUPER SELFIE!

Try the tips below for making your unique portrait and remember: A selfie doesn't always have to show your face. Be creative and also try capturing your best "faceless" self—the only kind of selfies that National Geographic Kids My Shot will post!

Supply List

- your camera
- you
- a mirror, window, or fun environment

STEPS

1. Be an original Have you ever noticed that most selfies are taken from the same angle—with the camera slightly above the head and pointing downward? Don't do it! "You want to stand out from the crowd," urges photo editor Lori Epstein. "Take a photo of your partial reflection in a mirror or even a window. Just be creative—without capturing your full face!"

2. Lighting Avoid using the flash or other bright lights that can make your face look washed out. Instead, opt for natural light when possible.

3. Don't be a poser If you're going to take a full-on face shot to share with your friends or family, don't try too hard to act too serious or too goofy when taking a selfie. You'll look best if you're being your natural awesome self.

MYSHOT User: TheOwl

4. Beware the photobomber Look around to make sure no one is standing behind you or will jump into your shot. There's nothing more lame than having your photo ruined by someone who's making a face in the background.

TAKE THE CHALLENGE

IF YOU'RE EAGER TO SHARE YOUR PHOTOS, try entering a photography contest—or start one up!—at your school, library, or nature club. National Geographic Kids My Shot has many inspiring categories, with contests and challenges to enter. There's even an international photo contest. My Shot experts review the photos that kids submit and award them with prizes. Entrants can collect more than 70 badges at ngkidsmyshot.com. Contests and challenges also inspire you and give you ideas about what to shoot. Check out some My Shot winners:

CHALLENGE: Earth Day

CHALLENGE: Collections

MYSHOT   User: RILEY21

MYSHOT   User: windycityballe

MYSHOT   User: ritterbit

MY SHOT User: DreamInColour

CATEGORIES: Animals and Pets

MY SHOT User: clickit

CATEGORY: Landscape

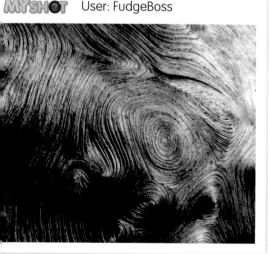

MY SHOT User: FudgeBoss

CATEGORY: Abstract

CAREERS FOR CAMERA HOUNDS

WHO: Jed Winer

JOB: Special Projects Assistant

Q What do you do as a special projects assistant?

A I work with the My Shot team to moderate content for the site. Kids upload photos and post comments all the time. I review the content before it's posted.

Q Sounds fun! How did you end up with this job?

A I started as an intern with National Geographic Television, then applied for this position. It wasn't as easy as it sounds. Lots of people want to work at National Geographic, so I feel lucky. It probably helped that my personal mission has been to inspire people to care about the planet, just like National Geographic's mission.

Q What career advice do you have for kids?

A Always keep people in mind. I stayed in touch with people I met during my internship to let them know I was interested. Also, be persistent! I applied for a lot of jobs before I got this one.

GET CRAFTY

THERE ARE NO LIMITS to what you can do with digital pictures, some craft supplies, and your imagination. For birthdays, holidays, and for your own enjoyment, you can frame your pictures, make greeting cards, create stationery, and so much more. Any local craft store will have the glue, paint, and framing materials you'll need.

Print It

The obvious thing to do with your images is to have them printed and framed. If you own a photo printer, you can do this at home—although the print may not last as long as a professionally printed one. Just make sure you use high-quality paper that's designed to hold photo printer ink to minimize smudging. Otherwise, you can have a photo lab do the work for you. Glossy photos look vibrant and reflective, while matte photos have no shine. If you're going to display your photos in a bright place, you may opt for matte so that glare won't be an issue.

Scrapbook It

Another way to show off your photos is to store them in a scrapbook. First, choose a journal or album. Next, select photos that reflect a theme or an event. It could be a holiday, a special dinner, or even a hike. Using double-sided tape or a photo-safe glue, stick the photos to a page. Decorate the page with markers or colored pencils. If you have special mementos from the event, stick them to the page as well. These can include pressed flowers, ticket stubs, ribbons, or leaf rubbings.

A FLOWERED FRAME CAN GO INTO A SCRAPBOOK OR HANG ON YOUR WALL.

Frame It

You don't need a photo lab to "frame" your photos in unique ways. Try turning your photos into place mats and coasters. Using a photo-friendly adhesive, glue your photos to a piece of construction paper. If you're making a place mat use a full piece of paper, but if you're making coasters, cut a piece of paper into a square or circle that's slightly larger than the radius of a cup. After the glue dries, have an adult help you cover both sides of the paper with a clear contact sheet and then trim the edges. Voilà!

MAKE A PHOTO CUBE!

Instead of a traditional picture frame, show off your photos in style with a photo cube. Photo cubes are easy to make—and make great gifts. Here's how:

Supply List

- a 4-inch square block of wood
- wax paper
- a regular paint brush
- acrylic paint (any color)
- a sponge paint brush
- clear sealant, such as Modge Podge
- 6 photos, trimmed to 3.5-inch squares
- spray-on sealant

STEPS

1. Place the wooden cube on a table that you've lined with wax paper.

2. Use the regular paint brush and acrylic paint to paint five sides of your cube. Place the cube down on the unpainted side and let it dry.

3. After the paint has dried, paint the unfinished side and let it dry.

4. Take your sponge paint brush and use it to apply the sealant to one side of the cube.

5. Press one photo to the sticky side of the cube and let it dry.

6. Repeat steps 4 and 5 with the remaining sides of the cube. You can do up to three sides at a time.

7. Next, cover each photo with two or three layers of the sealant.

8. After the cube is dry, apply a coat of spray-on sealant over all of the sides to prevent stickiness. Let the cube dry overnight.

6

EXPERT TIP

One great way to show off your photos is to have an art exhibition. Many cafés or libraries feature works from local artists. If this is true of your neighborhood café or library, ask the owner or manager if your work could be displayed. Otherwise, talk to your teacher or principal about having an exhibition at school.

—Laura Goertzel, My Shot team

SEEiNG THROUGH
THE LENS

What you see is what you get when it comes
to composing your scene. But sometimes
your photos don't appear as clear or as bright
as you want them to. In this chapter, we'll
explore why this happens—and what you can
do to get the photograph you want.

HUMAN EYE
VS. CAMERA EYE

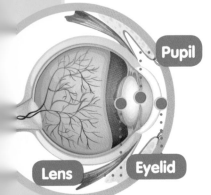

Pupil

Lens

Eyelid

IN SOME WAYS, THE HUMAN EYE is very much like a camera. It has a lens that focuses light reflected from objects, its pupil works like an aperture that allows light to enter, and its eyelid acts like a shutter. But human eyes are capable of doing something that the camera cannot: They can see in 3–D. In other words, they can perceive the length, depth, and height of objects.

YOU CAN FAKE A 3-D PHOTO!

Your camera probably can't take three-dimensional (3-D) photos, but you can create a 3-D illusion. Take a photo of multiple objects: one object in the foreground and the others set at different distances behind it. The foreground object will appear larger. Adding shadows to the background objects increases their depth, texture, and shape.

WHY DO WE SEE IN 3-D?

Hold one finger before your face and close your right eye. Then open your right eye and close your left. Your finger should appear to move from side to side. This illustrates how humans perceive 3-D objects: Each eye, spaced slightly apart, sees the world a bit differently. Your brain combines the images, forming one that's 3-D. Most cameras have only one lens, so don't see the world in 3-D.

DiD YOU KNOW?

IN THE 1840S, PHOTOGRAPHERS wanting to create a 3-D image took two similar photographs from different points of view. They placed them in a device called a stereoscope, which created the illusion of a 3-D image. In the mid-1900s, View-Masters took the place of stereoscopes for viewing scenic postcards in 3-D.

MAKE A 3-D ILLUSION!

You might be thinking, if cameras aren't capable of producing 3-D images then how are 3-D films made? The answer is simple: 3-D films are shot using two lenses that are placed beside each other, much like human eyes. They film the same scene, but from slightly different perspectives. When you watch the film, you wear special glasses that trick your brain into seeing the multiple images as one that is three-dimensional. To demonstrate this concept, try this optical-illusion activity.

Supply List

- a digital camera or smart-phone (preferably 2 phones)

STEPS

1. Take two photographs of the subject from different perspectives. If you have two smartphones, position them next to each other, facing the same direction, with the lenses as close as possible to one other. If you have just one camera, snap a photo and then move it over by three inches to take the second photo.

2. Print your images or upload them to your computer.

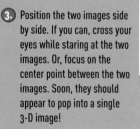

3. Position the two images side by side. If you can, cross your eyes while staring at the two images. Or, focus on the center point between the two images. Soon, they should appear to pop into a single 3-D image!

📷 EXPERT TIP

The illusion of depth in a photograph usually comes from shadows and highlights interacting on the subject. Photos will appear to have greater depth if the main light is coming from a low angle. That's a simple explanation for why experienced photographers tend to shoot their best pictures early in the morning or late in the afternoon.
—Dan Westergren, photo editor

AUTOFOCUS
LENS

WHEN YOU TAKE A PHOTO, IT'S IMPORTANT that your subject appears as sharp as possible so that viewers know what to focus on when they look at your pictures. Fortunately, most cameras come with an **autofocus** lens, which does the job for you.

WHAT YOU SHOULD KNOW

For cameras with a single focus point in the center, all you have to do is make sure your subject appears in the center of the camera's viewfinder and then press the shutter button halfway down. Your camera will highlight what is in focus in a box (usually green). Then continue pressing down to take the photo!

- **Fooling Your Camera** Suppose you don't want your subject to appear in the center of the frame. How do you do this and still keep the focus on the subject? One option is to turn off the autofocus feature and then manually focus your lens. However, not every camera has this option. To get around this problem, you can fool your autofocus lens. Here's how:

  - Position your subject in the viewfinder. Then, press the shutter button partway down and hold it there. This will lock the focus in on your subject.

  - Next, move your camera so that your subject is where you'd like it to appear in the frame. (Don't lift your finger up from the button!)

  - Press the shutter button all the way down. The result? Your subject will appear sharp even if it isn't in the center of the frame.

WHAT WENT WRONG?

EXPERT TIP

Try a smile-detection app on your smartphone. It detects a person by facial recognition and then focuses in and snaps the picture when it sees a smile.
—Kelley Miller, photo editor

In the left photo, the photographer wanted to focus on the chain. Yet the chain doesn't appear sharp. Instead, the harbor below does. What do you think went wrong?

NO

YES

MYSHOT   User: jayudhwani

autofocus:
a device that allows the camera to focus automatically on the subject in the viewfinder

75

ANNIE'S ASSIGNMENT

CHOOSING YOUR FOCUS

A SIMPLE WAY TO MAKE A PHOTO more artistic is to work with your aperture setting to control your depth of field. After you set your aperture, adjust your shutter speed to make a perfect exposure (see pages 78–81).

RAINDROPS ON PINE NEEDLES IN MINNESOTA

 User: RILEY21

FUN FACT

Remember, there is no *correct* way to select your aperture. It's a creative tool that you can use to make *your* favorite picture.

STEPS

1. A telephoto lens has less depth of field, so it's a great lens to use if you want just one thing in focus (selective focus). Find a garden nearby and use your longest lens to photograph the flowers. First, focus on one flower and close down your aperture to around f-11 or f-16. Now shoot the same flower with your aperture wide open (the smallest number you can use with your lens). Each time, be sure to set your shutter speed. Compare the differences among your two shots. The first shot should have more flowers in the garden in focus than the second shot. But you may like the second shot better, because the selective focus makes the single flower jump out of the background.

THE FLOWER IS IN FOCUS. SO IS THE WALKING STICK INSECT ABOVE IT!

2. Now choose your widest lens and try the same exercise. Wide-angle lenses have greater depth of field, so you will not see as dramatic a difference in a field of flowers. Now choose a simple subject, like a ball. Get low and photograph with your lens wide open. Focus only on the subject in the foreground and see what happens to the background. Next, shoot the same subject with the aperture closed down, and you will see a very different picture.

EXPERT TIP

Before cameras had great internal light meters, photographers used hand-held light meters and had to make choices about aperture and shutter speed for every shot. It helped us think more artistically about which settings to choose. The same artistry can happen with today's cameras, if you are willing to practice knowing what your aperture and shutter speeds will do. —Annie Griffiths

MYSHOT   User: snyrx

DEPTH OF FiELD

HAVE YOU EVER LOOKED AT A PHOTO in which the subject appears very sharp while other objects seem out of focus or blurry? This technique involves the use of depth of field to bring attention to a subject. **Depth of field** refers to the amount of a photo that is in focus. When only a small area of a photo is in focus, it has a "shallow" depth of field, whereas a photo that's completely in focus has a "deep" depth of field.

A LARGER APERTURE GIVES A SHALLOW DEPTH OF FIELD, MAINLY KEEPING THE SUBJECT IN FOCUS.

depth of field: the area within a photograph that is in focus

shallow depth of field

A SMALLER APERTURE GIVES A DEEP DEPTH OF FIELD, WITH MORE OF THE ENTIRE IMAGE IN FOCUS.

deep depth of field

EXPERT TIP

The lens you use helps determine the depth of field. A telephoto lens has less depth of field than a regular lens; a wide-angle lens has greater depth of field (see page 77).

—Annie Griffiths

WHAT YOU SHOULD KNOW

The aperture is the lens opening that lets light in. The smaller the hole, the less light that passes through. A narrower aperture creates a sharper photo overall, with greater depth of field. A wider aperture lets in more light but results in shallower depth of field.

f-stop:
the number that indicates the size of the lens opening, or aperture

F → 1 1.4 2 2.8 4 5.6 8 11 16 22 32

- **About Apertures** Apertures are measured in units called **f-stops**. Some lenses have these units along the barrel.

- **What Those Crazy Numbers Mean** The f-stops are the size of the aperture, or lens opening. You adjust your f-stop to make the opening bigger (a smaller f-stop number) or to make it smaller (a larger f-stop number).

- **What the Numbers Do** By choosing a lower f-stop number, you're widening your aperture. This will let in more light but allow fewer things to be in focus. A higher f-stop number will result in a smaller opening, letting in less light and allowing a larger area of your photo to be in focus.

- **Why the Numbers Are Important** They work together with shutter speed to give your photo the right exposure!

- **How the Numbers Work Together** Aperture alone can't give you the right exposure. The aperture number needs to work hand in hand with the shutter speed: See how this happens on the next page.

- **Solutions for Point-and-Shoot Cameras** If you have a point-and-shoot camera, you may not be able to see the range of f-stops. You can still adjust your aperture with shooting modes such as landscape and portrait (see the modes on page 150).

MYSHOT User: nepalgirl

"I loved the pattern and shapes these petals made, and I thought the colors would pop.

"The petals looked like a salsa dancer's dress. The shallow depth of field let me focus on that pattern without much in the background.

"I think it's successful. I've learned that when I take a photo I don't like, I can think of how to make it better, and test it out. Practice helps."

SHUTTER SPEED

APERTURE IS JUST ONE OF TWO CONTROLS that determine how much light will enter your camera. Shutter speed, or the time during which the shutter is open, also plays a role. Aperture and shutter speed work together to create "exposure"—the amount of light that enters the camera.

slow shutter speed

fast shutter speed

EXPERT TIP

Get to know how steady you are by practicing with different lenses and shutter speeds. You may be steady as a rock with a wide-angle lens at a 60th of a second, but everything is blurry at that speed with a big telephoto. The only way to know is to practice. Try hand-holding your lenses at different shutter speeds. It will help you know your limits and have fewer blurry pictures! Remember, if you need a faster shutter speed you can sometimes adjust your aperture—and you can always adjust your ISO! (See pages 36 and 150.) —Annie Griffiths

WHAT YOU SHOULD KNOW

All the numbers for shutter speeds and apertures can get confusing. The main thing you need to know is that these two settings work together to let in the right amount of light to give a proper exposure. If you change one, you need to change the other. Fully automatic cameras do this for you. As you grow more experienced, you can make more artistic choices! (See page 150 for creative camera modes.)

> **shutter speed:**
> the length of time the shutter is open, letting light reach the sensor. A slow shutter speed lets in more light; a fast speed lets in less light.

- **About Shutter Speed** Shutter speed is measured in fractions of seconds, so 250 on your shutter speed means the shutter is only open for 1/250 of a second. The larger the fraction denominator, the faster that shutter is moving! Very slow shutters speeds of 1 second or more will appear as 1", 10", etc., instead of as a fraction.

- **Fast vs. Slow** Faster shutter speeds allow you to freeze motion. This is great for capturing a crisp, detailed image of a moving object. Slower shutter speeds do the opposite—they allow a fast-moving object to blur. This is handy if you want to emphasize the motion or speed of an object.

- **Aperture + Shutter Speed = Exposure** Both the shutter speed number, or setting, and the aperture number allow light to enter the camera. That means the numbers have to work together to give you the right amount of light for your exposure. Think about it: If you change your aperture so that the aperture hole is bigger, then your shutter must move quicker, or too much light will get in.

- **The Right Exposure** Most digital cameras can automatically select the correct aperture and shutter speed, but sometimes a camera gets it wrong. If your photo is dark, or "underexposed," or light, or "overexposed," turn on exposure compensation (see below) before you shoot again. It's labeled with a +/- sign. Plus adds light; minus decreases light.

MYSHOT

User: Truthpower

"The light outside was beautiful. I had a camera, a subject, and a small idea.

"I put my camera on a tripod, used a timer, and stood before it with the pinwheel. Gradually I lowered the shutter speed from 1/80 of a second to 1/8. Each time, I stepped closer and spun the pinwheel faster.

"Slowing the shutter speed is like painting—surreal. At last the image was out of my head, into the camera."

CAPTURING LIGHT QUALITY

THE QUALITY OF LIGHT USED TO TAKE A PICTURE is just as important as the amount of light used. What do we mean by quality? The light needs to be flattering to your subject, create a certain atmosphere or mood, and, if possible, make the objects in your photo appear three-dimensional.

WHAT YOU SHOULD KNOW

In general, there are two types of light—hard light and soft light. Each has different qualities.

- **Hard Light** Hard light usually comes from a small light source. This may include a small light bulb or direct sunlight. Hard light tends to produce bright highlights that can help a colorful subject, like a red tomato or a yellow sunflower, really pop. The downside is that hard light can cast a lot of shadows—and that can be unflattering to human subjects and cause you to lose important details. In addition, if the light is too intense, it may cause glare on a reflective surface, such as a glass building.

- **Soft Light** Soft light comes from a large, scattered light source and tends to wrap around your subject. One example is the light on a cloudy day. Soft light doesn't cast deep shadows so it's great for photographing people and capturing details. One exception to the rule is the soft light visible during hazy or misty days. During such times, particles in the air filter the light. This can make colors look like pastels and reduce sharpness, so fewer details are visible.

hard light

soft light

SUNFLOWERS ON A SUNNY DAY   SUNFLOWERS ON AN OVERCAST DAY

WHAT WENT WRONG?

In what kind of light did the photographer take these pictures?
Which light is better to display the building?

NO

YES

DID YOU KNOW?

ARTISTS UNDERSTOOD THE EFFECTS of light long before photography was invented. During the height of the Renaissance period in the 15th century, many artists used chiaroscuro—a technique that involves light and shading—to create a three-dimensional effect in their paintings.

83

ANNiE'S
ASSiGNMENT

BALANCING TWILIGHT WITH AMBIENT LIGHT

HAVE YOU EVER NOTICED THAT MAGIC TIME about 30 minutes after sunset when lights come on in buildings and the sky becomes deep blue? It's one of the most wonderful times to photograph an evening scene. All you need is a tripod and a little bit of patience to make a beautiful long exposure, also called a time exposure.

THE LIGHTS COME ON IN AN AMUSEMENT PARK IN SYDNEY, AUSTRALIA.

tungsten:
a chemical element used in electric lights to make them glow

FUN FACT
The reason the colors are so beautiful in a twilight exposure is because the camera doesn't adjust to the different colors of artificial light the way our eyes automatically do. So the true yellows of **tungsten** light perfectly complement the blue of the night sky.

TWILIGHT AT A HOTEL IN TURKEY

STEPS

1. Find a scene that will have artificial light in the evening. It's especially nice if there are inside and outside lights that come on after the sun goes down.

2. Arrive before sunset to set up your tripod and composition. To make a long exposure, you will control the exposure by setting your aperture first (for most scenes you can have it wide open), and then using only your shutter speed to adjust for the changing light.

3. For a short period, just after sunset, things can look pretty dull, but be patient while the sky darkens and the artificial lights start to come on. Watch carefully for the moment that the intensity of the artificial light begins to match the natural light. It happens in an instant, so start clicking as soon as the balance gets close and continue clicking for a bit after the artificial light becomes brighter than the sky. Magic!

4. Remember that some skies are less colorful than others, so you may need to try this technique more than once to get the best image.

📷 EXPERT TIP

When you plan your composition for a twilight shot, keep in mind that large empty spaces where there are no lights or sky can distract from the final image. This is easy to forget when you are composing before the lights come on. —Annie Griffiths

QUALITY OF DAYLIGHT

THROUGHOUT THE DAY, THE SUN'S POSITION in the sky changes—and with each new position, so does the quality of light. In general, light may seem yellow or pink at sunrise, but by midday, when the sun is highest in the sky, the light appears a neutral white. Between midafternoon and sunset, the light gradually becomes more orange. For a better idea of how light changes throughout the day, check out the photos shown here.

ARCHES NATIONAL PARK, MOAB, UTAH

DID YOU KNOW?

THE FIRST HOUR OF LIGHT AFTER SUNRISE and the last hour of light before sunset are each called the "golden hour" by photographers. During these times the sun is low in the sky so it produces a soft light that flatters just about any subject.

MAKE A COLOR WHEEL!

The sun's light seems white, so why does it look different throughout the day? Believe it or not, white light is made of seven different colors: red, orange, yellow, green, blue, indigo, and violet. If this sounds familiar, it's because these are the seven colors of a rainbow. Throughout the day, the sun's angle in the sky and the conditions of the atmosphere change. This causes some colors to become more visible than others. For a better understanding of how these different colors form white light, try this activity.

Supply List
- a paper plate
- scissors
- a pencil
- a ruler
- 7 crayons or markers in each of the following colors: red, orange, yellow, green, blue, indigo, and violet

STEPS

1. Cut off the outer rim of the paper plate with a pair of scissors. After you are done, you should be left with a flat circle.

2. Think of your circle as a pie. Using a pencil and a ruler, draw seven equal pie slices on the circle.

3. Color each slice with a different crayon or marker.

4. Use your pencil to punch a hole in the center of the circle.

5. Stick the tip of your pencil through the hole, so that your eraser is about one inch above the colors of the wheel.

6. Grab the part of the pencil that lies below the wheel in between your hands. Spin the pencil as fast as you can.

What color do you see? The color you should have seen is white. Why? As you spin the wheel quickly, your eyes combine all the colors in the wheel. When the seven colors combine, they form white. If you didn't see it, try securing the wheel to the pencil with tape so the wheel doesn't slip and can spin faster—and try again!

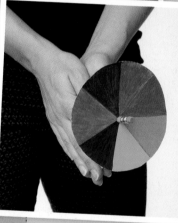

📷 EXPERT TIP

Light is usually best around sunrise and sunset because it's softer and often has more color. When the sun is low, its light travels through more dust or moisture particles on the horizon. Those particles refract, or split, the light and create color. —Annie Griffiths

LiGHTiNG DiRECTiONS

YOU'VE LEARNED THAT THE QUALITY OF NATURAL LIGHT changes from sunrise to sunset. Though some of this has to do with the changing conditions of the atmosphere throughout the day, the sun's actual position in the sky also has an effect. The information holds true for indoor lights.

Front Lighting

What happens when you stare directly into a light source? You squint! The same will happen if you photograph a person or animal when the light source is in the front. If this isn't an issue for you—or your subject—go for it. Why? Front lighting isn't all that bad. It casts warm hues, which is great for skin tones. It's also the perfect light for capturing details.

Top Lighting

When a light source, such as the sun, is directly above the subject, it creates short, dark shadows. If you're taking pictures of an unusually shaped object, this can be very appealing because the shadow patterns will be dramatic. The effect will be equally dramatic on humans, but not in a good way. Top lighting tends to make eye sockets look dark and causes chins to cast weird, unflattering shadows.

Side Lighting

When the sun is low in the sky or a lamp is positioned to the side, it illuminates half of your subject and casts the rest in shadows. If your subject is a person, this can be an excellent way to convey his or her emotions—and thus create a mood in your photo. Side lighting also casts long shadows, which can help emphasize the depth and texture of landscapes. (We'll explain this further in the next section.) The only downside to side lighting is that you won't be able to see much detail in the shadowy areas. You can enhance the image by positioning a piece of white poster board so that the light bounces back onto the shadowy side of your subject.

Back Lighting

You've probably seen many photos of silhouettes. These are dark shapes and outlines of people or things. These images are taken when the light source is behind the subject. As you can imagine, back lighting is an excellent way to capture the shape of an object, but like side lighting, it isn't ideal for details.

EXPERT TIP

Back lighting is one of my favorite lighting styles. It can provide soft light in a subject's hair, enhance autumn colors, or create a powerful silhouette. The key is to think about your exposure: Too light an exposure loses the drama of the backlight. Too dark an exposure will create a silhouette. —Annie Griffiths

CAREERS FOR CAMERA HOUNDS

WHO: Mark Thiessen

JOB: Staff Photographer, National Geographic

Q What kind of photos do you take for National Geographic?

A I specialize in photographing subjects in places where light is a challenge.

Q What are some lighting challenges you've encountered?

A I've photographed microbes under the ice in Antarctica. I also took photos of *Titanic* director James Cameron when he began a mission to the deepest part of the ocean aboard a submersible. Both were dark environments.

Q How did you get into photography?

A When I was 14, my mom got me a radio to listen in on fire-emergency calls. She'd drive me to the scene of the fire, and I'd take pictures. A local newspaper published one of my photos on the front page!

Q Do you still photograph fire?

A Yes! It's what I'm known for. I've taken photos of many forest fires and even rappelled out of airplanes with smokejumpers in Russia. Fire safety courses have helped me face dangerous situations.

Q What advice would you give to kids who are interested in this job?

A Start taking photos now!

SHADOW PLAY

SHADOWS CAN BE A PHOTOGRAPHER'S BEST FRIEND! As you read in the previous section, they can make an ordinary subject more interesting by creating a mood. They can also help emphasize various characteristics of an object to give a three-dimensional appearance.

▶ DEPTH AND TEXTURE

Painters often use shading to emphasize the depth and texture of objects. This gives a flat artwork the illusion of being three-dimensional. A terraced field (below), already has texture, but shadows captured in a photograph can make the texture look more defined. Check out this image of footprints in the sand (right), taken in late afternoon when the sun was low in the sky. Notice how the shadow accentuates the footprints?

FOOTPRINTS IN THE SAND, MOZAMBIQUE (ABOVE); A TERRACED RICE FIELD IN SAPA, VIETNAM (LEFT)

THE SHAPE OF THINGS

Shadows can also be a great way to emphasize the shape of an object. Let's say you want to take a photo of a metal gate. There's nothing special about the color, but the design is interesting. You can capture this by focusing your camera on the subject's shadow. However, make sure that the shadow appears against a plain background—such as a snowy bank, a grassy field, a dirt road, or a wall with nothing on it. Otherwise, it may compete with other elements in the frame.

📷 EXPERT TIP

Shadows can add an extra element to your photos and sometimes even be the subject of the picture. You usually have to be careful to avoid your own shadow, because it can be distracting. But the shadow of someone unseen in the picture can add an element of mystery.
—Annie Griffiths

MYSHOT User: bayernmunichrules

"I love this image for its lessons about the power of light," says Your Shot editor Marie McGrory.

"First, you have warm light coming through the translucent ball, showing its details.

"Then you have shadows that block out the rest of the frame, spotlighting the ball.

"Finally, you have a little light magic as the sun pours through the ball's center, leaving a sparkle in the middle of the shadow."

91

ANNiE'S ASSiGNMENT

LONG EXPOSURES

THE BEST PART OF PHOTOGRAPHING FIREWORKS is that no two shots are alike! Each shot is a time-varied exposure, and you get to decide how long to keep the shutter open as you watch the exploding sky.

FIREWORKS OVER WASHINGTON, D.C.

MYSHOT   User: melqwe

FUN FACT

On July 4, keep your camera ready! More than 14,000 firework displays light up the sky across the United States.

TRY YOUR OWN: **LONG EXPOSURES**

Try capturing Fourth of July fireworks in your neighborhood using this technique.

STEPS

1. Secure the camera tightly to a tripod and attach a remote release cord if you have one. (The cord keeps the camera from moving while you make your time exposure.)

2. If you don't have a release cord, practice depressing the shutter slowly and carefully for each shot.

3. Fireworks are brighter than you think, so set your ISO to 400 and your lens f-stop to f-5.6 or f-8 for a wider aperture. (See pages 36, 79, and 150 for more about ISO and f-stops.)

4. Be creative with shutter speed. Exposures can vary from a few seconds to more than 30 seconds if you use the bulb setting. This keeps the shutter open as long as the shutter button is held down. After you've captured enough bursts, release the button.

5. Try to avoid looking at the back of the camera more than once or twice, and then just look quickly to see if the exposure looks good. Remember, you might miss the best shot if you are looking at your last shot.

EXPERT TIP

Think about your composition as you set up your tripod. Pictures of fireworks are usually more interesting if there is something in the picture that stands still, such as a building or a statue. Use a self-timer if your hands are shaking. Try the fireworks setting as a preset mode.
—Annie Griffiths

MY SHOT   User: Bagman

iNDOOR LiGHTiNG

WHEN YOU TAKE PICTURES INDOORS during the day, you can make use of natural light streaming through windows. Window light is especially flattering for portraits and appears natural in photos. But what happens after the sun goes down or if you're taking photos in a windowless room? You'll most likely have to rely on artificial light. In general, there are three types of artificial light: incandescent, fluorescent, and halogen. Each produces a different color—and a different challenge.

WHAT YOU SHOULD KNOW

- **Incandescent** Incandescent light bulbs, which are popular in homes, contain a filament that heats up and produces light with the help of an electrical current. These lights cast a warm yellow tone in photographs.

- **Halogen** Some incandescent bulbs contain halogen elements. These halogen bulbs are brighter than the regular incandescent variety and aren't as warm colored. If you're shooting a subject against a white background under halogen lights, your photo may have a greenish tint.

- **Fluorescent** If you've ever been to a sporting event or set foot inside a gym you know how bright fluorescent lighting can be. But unless you've tried taking photos in such an environment, you probably don't know the challenges it can create. Fluorescent lighting is harsh—and it makes your photos look green!

FIX THOSE CRAZY COLORS

You might be wondering why your camera is capturing these colors incorrectly. After all, they look normal to you. The answer is that your eyes have the ability to adjust to different lights and can therefore see things correctly. The same doesn't hold true for your camera. So, can anything be done to make your photos look more natural? Yes! It involves something called white balance.

- **White Balance** This is a feature in your camera that adjusts colors so that they look natural in your photo. You can set this feature to work automatically. Use the setting labeled AWB (Automatic White Balance). It allows your camera to read a scene's color temperature and choose the setting that will give you the truest color (see page 150).

- **White Balance Settings** Cameras aren't perfect, so even if your white balance is set to automatic, the colors may still turn out weird. If this happens, you'll need to adjust the white balance setting to offset the light source in the room. For example, if you're shooting under fluorescent lights, choose the fluorescent setting. Meanwhile, the tungsten setting works wonders for incandescent and halogen lights.

WITH WHITE BALANCE

WITHOUT WHITE BALANCE

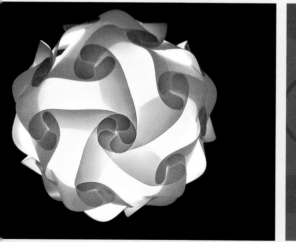

MYSHOT
User: volleyballgirl1

"Shooting into a light source usually creates a washed-out picture," says NG Kids photo editor Kelley Miller. But here the light is a beautiful lamp shade glowing against the black background.

"volleyballgirl1 corrected the camera's white balance to filter out unwanted yellow tones typical of this indoor light— so the lamp shade appears truer to its actual colors: white and pink. The photo has simplicity and symmetry."

EXPERT TIP

Mixed lighting sources can be interesting—or disastrous! Each kind of artificial light has a color that our eyes adjust for but that the camera sees more brightly. Lamplight is a warm yellow. Florescent and halogen lights are greenish. Try a flash so the main subject is not a bizarre shade of green. Or just have fun with the colors! —Annie Griffiths

FLASH

WHEN YOU WANT TO TAKE A PHOTO INSIDE A DIMLY LIT ROOM, the first thing you probably think of is flash. A flash is a brief burst of light that is built into most cameras. It is most often used to brighten dark areas, but it has other uses as well. For example, when you photograph someone in the middle of a bright sunny day, the sunlight may cast an ugly shadow on your subject's face. The light from your flash can fill in the shadows for a more normal look. Pretty cool, right? Still, it's not a good idea to use your flash every time because it can look unnatural.

▶ THE RED-EYE SYNDROME

We've all taken photos of people whose eyes were turned red by the glare of the flash. The red color is caused by a direct flash bouncing off the back of the subject's eyes. How do you avoid this problem? By using indirect light. If you can, take your flash off of the camera so that it's less direct. Or swivel the flash head so the light bounces off the ceiling or a wall. If that isn't possible, position your subject near another light source, such as a lamp. The extra light should help reduce red eye. Use the flash setting for red-eye reduction, which emits a beam that closes the pupils before the flash is fired. Also, external flashes are less likely to cause red eye.

▶ THE LIGHT AND DARK SIDE OF FLASH

Light from a flash is like sound from a speaker. The farther away your subject is, the softer the light is when it reaches the subject. So if you use your flash while in the audience at a hockey game, the light will never even reach the subject.

WHAT WENT WRONG?

In this photo, some of the people are well lit, but others are in the dark. Can you figure out what went wrong?

HARSH LIGHTING

The light from a flash can be really harsh. If you're using a camera with an external, adjustable flash, you can minimize this effect by adjusting the direction of the flash so that it isn't aimed directly at your subjects. Instead, aim the flash at a nearby wall or ceiling. This will make it look more like regular room lighting. On most cameras you can adjust the power, or intensity, of your flash.

DID YOU KNOW?

IN THE EARLY DAYS OF PHOTOGRAPHY, electronic flash equipment had not yet been invented. Photographers used a special flash powder instead. The powder was placed on a tray and then ignited to produce a brief flash of light. Needless to say, it was dangerous and created a lot of smoke.

NiGHT PHOTOGRAPHY

MOST PEOPLE DON'T THINK ABOUT TAKING PHOTOS AT NIGHT without a flash. And sure, nighttime isn't ideal for taking detailed photos of people or pets. But it's a terrific opportunity to take pictures of nighttime objects that emit their own light, such as stars, fireworks, and more.

Shoot for the Stars

Stars emit light, but you'll need a little help to capture as much of it as possible. To do this, choose the widest aperture on your camera and opt for a slow shutter speed. And remember, the slower speed means your shutter will stay open longer. So use a tripod. If you keep your shutter open, you'll capture star trails as the stars move.

Campfire

First rule: Never get too close to fire. You not only risk getting burned, but you can damage your camera as well. Now that we've gotten that out of the way, let's turn our attention to taking photos of those cozy campground embers. If you find that the fire and people closest to it look washed out, try underexposing the picture. Your camera's meter may be fooled by the dark sky. To take photos of a friend sitting near the campfire, have someone shine a flashlight in his or her face to help your camera focus.

"This photo shows a great combination of simplicity, lighting, and portraiture," says NG Kids photo editor Kelley Miller.

"The backlight from something like a flashlight outlines the person's profile. I love the detail in the wisps of hair.

"The backlight also lets us see the steam from his exhale and imagine the cold air. This illustrates the photo's title 'Midnight Hike,' and is a creative way to photograph a friend."

Night Lights

When glowing lights come on at DisneyWorld or other theme parks at night, you can capture an image as colorful as fireworks. First set your camera on a tripod. If your camera has a bulb mode, use it. The bulb setting will keep the shutter open as long as you hold the shutter button down. As the lights shimmer, open the shutter for as long as you like, and then release the button. Repeat this throughout the evening, trying both longer and shorter exposures.

DID YOU KNOW?

THE ALBUQUERQUE INTERNATIONAL BALLOON FIESTA, a popular hot-air balloon festival in New Mexico, has been called "the world's most photographed event." It is estimated that more than 25 million photos of the balloons have been taken during a single festival. Photographers gather before sunrise to capture the start of the festivities as the balloons launch into the dark predawn sky.

ANNiE'S ASSIGNMENT

TURN A FLASHLIGHT INTO A PHOTO PAINTBRUSH

PUT A LITTLE ZING INTO A QUIET SUBJECT by photographing it at night with a small flashlight. All you need is a tripod, a flashlight, complete darkness, and some long time exposures. Let the fun begin!

THE MILKY WAY OVER A MONGOLIAN GER (HOME)

FUN FACT

Using a flashlight to "paint" a night scene can look really spooky and is fun to try with gravestones in a cemetery. Just don't go alone!

STEPS

1. You will need a good tripod, a shutter-release cable, and a penlight or small flashlight. Be sure to read your camera's manual so that you understand how to keep your shutter open for long periods of time.

2. Choose a subject that doesn't move, like a statue or a cool rock, and choose a location where there are no lights. Then set up your tripod and your composition before it gets really dark. Set your aperture wide open—to the smallest f-stop.

3. When it gets very dark, open your shutter and use your flashlight like a paintbrush, moving it back and forth quickly over the subject for one minute, then five minutes, even ten minutes! Look at the resulting images to see what kind of exposure looks best to you. Then repeat the process at that exposure many times. Each shot will be unique because the light will move differently each time. This kind of light is far more interesting than if you just shoot it with your camera flash.

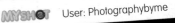 User: Photographybyme

📷 **EXPERT TIP**

It's tempting to always use your flash to light a dark scene, but natural, imperfect light can be far more interesting. Light that moves, like candle light, is lovely and a camera flash will completely destroy the mood.
—Annie Griffiths

SECRETS
OF THE TRADE

TRICKY LIGHTING SITUATIONS

JOEL SARTORE IS A WELL-KNOWN PHOTOGRAPHER who enjoys taking pictures of endangered wildlife around the world. Since most wildlife are active at dawn and dusk, Joel knows a thing or two about difficult lighting situations.

Q1 **What's one of your biggest challenges where lighting is concerned?**

Light always varies, whether you're indoors or outside. Most of the time it's pretty rough. So my challenge is to create lighting that's beautiful, lyrical, and simple enough to get the reader to pay attention to my subjects.

Q2 **Is there ever a time when the light outside is just right?**

Sure! Right after sunset on a clear day in the eastern horizon—not the western horizon, where the sun is setting. The east is washed in a soft orange or pink light, and shadows are illuminated. It's just beautiful and it makes everyone look their best.

Q3 How do you create light that's "beautiful" when you're outside?

Let's say you're taking pictures outside in the middle of a sunny day. Bright light shining down on a person's face will cause their brows to cast dark shadows around their eyes. They'll look like they're wearing a raccoon mask! They'll be squinting, too—and that's not fun for anyone. To get around this situation, you may ask them to move into the shade, where the light isn't shining directly on them. Or, if there is no shade, you can turn on your flash to fill in some of the shadows. But be careful. You don't want your subjects to look too lit. The lighting should be pretty and pleasing to the eye.

Q4 Can indoor lighting be flattering, too?

Yes, it can. Ambient lighting in a room can be a nice way to light a photo. Tungsten light [used for many lamps] creates a warm glow that can be flattering.

Q5 Suppose I'm at a birthday party, where the only light source is the light from the flickering candles on a cake. Can I use my flash?

I wouldn't do that. Direct light from a flash is really harsh and can make your picture look like a crime-scene photo! Instead, use any light that's available—in this case, the low light emitted from the birthday candles. If your camera can't handle low light, move closer to the subject. If it's too dark and you need to use flash—aim the light at a wall or ceiling to minimize the effect.

Q6 Does the same rule apply to indoor events like concerts?

Absolutely. Today, most concerts are well lit, so taking photos might not be as difficult as you think—especially if you're close to the stage.

Q7 But what if you have back-row seats?

If you're in the back row and can't get a good photo without flash, you may have to cut your losses. I always say that good photography is about what you exclude. And you need to exclude bad light!

YOUR BEST
SHOT

Mastering the controls of a camera is an important part of photography—but it isn't everything. Recognizing the details and angles that work together to create beautiful photos is also key. In this section of the book, we'll explore the art of photography.

COMPOSiTiON

IT'S NOT JUST WHAT YOU SHOOT, IT'S HOW YOU SHOOT IT

TODAY'S CAMERAS ARE VERY SOPHISTICATED. All you have to do is aim and press the shutter button, and the camera does the rest. However, there is something a camera can't do for you. It cannot *compose* the photo.

Good composition is about presenting the objects you photograph in a pleasing and artistic way. Why is this important? A poorly composed photo can make an exciting subject look boring. A well-composed photo can transform an ordinary subject into an extraordinary one.

good composition:
ideal arrangement of the subject and its surroundings in a frame

good composition

bad composition

WHAT YOU SHOULD KNOW

HOW TO COMPOSE A PHOTO

If you don't consider yourself artistic, don't worry. There are a few easy rules you can follow to get a good composition—and they involve asking yourself a few guiding questions:

- What is the subject?
- How do I frame the subject?
- How much of the frame should the subject fill?
- How does the subject relate to any objects in the background?

MYSHOT User: Erika

"The photo shows a room in my community in South Korea where families gather to remember loved ones who have died in recent wars.

"I wanted to avoid the families' faces to respect them because they are sad, so I told their story another way: by showing these very old chairs and photographs, many of them faded.

"When a pet cat came into the frame, it made the picture more loving."

EXPERT TIP

When composing, take a second to make sure there isn't anything distracting in the picture: a power line, a person in the background looking at you, a piece of trash. Try to change your angle to eliminate those distracting elements.
—Annie Griffiths

107

THE MAIN ATTRACTION

WHETHER IT'S A HOLIDAY PORTRAIT of your family or an image of your school soccer's team—every photo should have at least one thing in common: a subject, the main topic of the photograph. The subject is the person, pet, place, or action that will catch the viewer's eye.

When I look at some of the old photographs I've taken, I can't figure out what they're about.

Solution: Chances are that when you took the photo, you didn't stop to consider what you were trying to capture. Let that be a lesson. Before snapping a photo, always ask yourself, *What is my subject?* Subjects can be just about anything—people, animals, plants, architecture, and landscapes. Sometimes, they can even be shapes, colors, and emotions.

subject:
the main topic of a photograph

MYSHOT   User: Erika

WHAT WENT WRONG?

Check out the beach scene captured in this photo. What's wrong with it? What could the photographer have done to make it better?

The subject of my photo is obvious, but it still looks dull.

Solution: After you've picked a subject, figure out what you want to convey about it. In other words, ask yourself why you're photographing it. Sometimes, the answer is obvious, like when you want to capture how silly your kid sister looks wearing your mom's shoes, or how delicious those cupcakes look (right)! But other times, it's more subtle, like when you want to capture an emotion or a mood at an event. Regardless of your reason for photographing a subject, it should be obvious to anyone who views your photograph.

EXPERT TIP

Anything can be a good subject. I've seen lovely photographs of carrots! What matters is to pay attention to what your eye is attracted to. Sometimes it's a face or a color or a graphic element. The important thing is to follow your gut and spend some time looking for the perfect way to photograph the subject that your eye chooses. ——Annie Griffiths

FRAMING
YOUR SHOT

WHEN YOU HEAR THE WORD "FRAME," you might think of the wooden, metal, or plastic border that holds a painting or a photo. Frames not only help display the artwork, they also draw the viewer's attention to it. This same concept can be applied to photo composition. When you snap a photo, you can use objects from the scenery to frame—and thus draw attention to—your subject. These objects can include trees, buildings, archways, windows, doorways, and more.

good framing

DID YOU KNOW?

OVER THE YEARS, MANY FAMOUS PAINTERS have had picture frames designed to complement their artwork. Some felt so strongly about the frame's ability to enhance their painting that they went to great lengths to ensure it would never be removed. Georges Seurat would paint the frame, James McNeill Whistler would sign the frame instead of the painting, and Edgar Degas would threaten to buy his artwork back from anyone who replaced the frame he had chosen.

HOT SHOT: Jimmy Chin

In climbing photography, I focus on three things: 1) Safety. 2) Showcasing the climber and their body position or facial expressions. 3) Putting the climber in the context of their environment. I often place the subject using the rule of thirds (see page 118) for the most impact.

WHAT YOU SHOULD KNOW

Consider your subject when choosing framing devices. Your frame should complement the subject, not compete with it for attention. For example, if you want to take a serene-looking photo of a horse in a meadow, you wouldn't want to use graffiti-covered walls as a frame; it would clash too much with the otherwise peaceful scene. The busy quality of the walls would also take attention away from the horse. Instead, tree branches or flowers would be more appropriate.

bad framing

📷 EXPERT TIP

Once you've made a photograph in which your subject is framed by its surroundings, you'll need a physical frame to show it off. The size of the matte—the cardboard border—between the image and the physical frame is key. It allows the picture to float. A small image can look more artful with a wider matte behind it.

—Annie Griffiths

MOVE iN FOR A CLOSER SHOT!

WHEN MOST PEOPLE TAKE PICTURES they make the mistake of capturing more than they need. As a result, the subject becomes lost in the busy background and the photo looks like it's lacking a focal point. Don't let this happen to you! Give your subject the attention it deserves by moving in for a closer shot.

How can I make sure my subject is the main focus of the photograph?

Solution: Getting closer to your subject not only ensures that it will be the focus of your photograph, but it also gives you a chance to capture important details that you'd lose if you were standing far away, such as the freckles of a person's face, an acorn dangling from a tree, or a bee pollinating a flower.

... But Not Too Close
Get to know your camera to learn how close you can focus. If it is blurry, you may be closer than the lens is capable of focusing.

Tools of the Trade
What if you want to take a photo of an animal at the zoo? Or a car on a race track? Let's face it: Sometimes it just isn't possible to get close to a subject. In these situations, you need a little help:

- For a superclose shot you might want to try a **macro lens**. Some can magnify objects up to five times their size.
- **Close-up filters** are also available. These filters are like magnifying glasses that you attach to the lens. The filters come in sets of three—each produces a different level of magnification.
- Most point-and-shoot cameras have an **optical zoom**. The zoom adjusts the camera lens to move in for a closer shot.

CAREERS FOR CAMERA HOUNDS

WHO: Darlyne Murawski **JOB:** Macro Photographer

Q What inspired you to pursue this line of work?

A When I was a child, I loved the photography in *National Geographic* and had a favorite photographer/author, Paul Zahl. Paul was both a biologist and a nature photographer. However, at that time, I had no idea I could aspire to do something like that.

Q What types of subjects do you photograph?

A I photograph all kinds of subjects, but mostly things from nature—like animals, plants, and fungi. I don't have one favorite. Whatever I'm photographing at the time seems to be my favorite. Last summer it was dragonflies.

Q What type of equipment do you use to get such close shots of your subjects?

A For extreme close-ups, I have used microscopes [e.g., a scanning electron microscope, a light microscope, a dissecting microscope]. Using my SLR camera, I have attached close-up tubes to my macro lenses to get super close [to subjects such as dust mites]. In that situation, you need LOTS of bright light.

Q Has anything unusual ever happened while shooting these creatures?

A Unexpected things happen all the time in the field: A monkey stole my lunch from my backpack; a poisonous coral snake slid by my knees while I was busy photographing a spider in Costa Rica; a squid inked me; a tree frog kept jumping onto my camera lens while I was trying to get its picture. And one of the latest: I fell into the Bay of Fundy at low tide and got covered in silt—and needed to be rescued. I've got creepy crocodile stories, too.

Q What advice would you give to kids who are interested in macro photography?

A Patience, perseverance, and a love of your subject matter. Also, get a camera with a macro lens that lets you get up close to your subject and make it look really large. Hold the camera still while you shoot. Consider what angle makes your subject look its best. Learn how to focus on your subject. You might need to focus manually [not autofocus]. Be very careful with the focusing so that you get a sharp image.

MYSHOT User: Vinyonga

ANNIE'S ASSIGNMENT

CAPTURE THE LIGHT IN THEIR EYES!

WE'VE ALL HEARD THE PHRASE "A LIGHT IN HER EYES," but did you know that capturing that light is a key to great portraiture? The small glimmer in a person's eye is called a "catch light," and it makes any portrait feel more intimate.

A TODDLER MAKES A FORT OUT OF HER BLANKET.

FUN FACT

Movie audiences tend to feel that eyes without catch lights are lifeless or evil, so filmmakers will eliminate catch lights in the "bad guys" eyes!

STEPS

1. Choose a friend to be your model, because practicing this will take a little time.

2. This technique works best with a telephoto lens, but it can be done with a wide-angle lens, too.

3. Find a spot out of the sun, preferably in open shade, and compose a nice head-and-shoulders portrait. A spot close to a window will work, too.

4. Once you have your shot set up, ask your subject to move only his or her eyes around slowly. You may need to direct them by moving a finger around and asking them to follow it with their eyes. As soon as you see the light reflecting, ask them to stop and continue looking in that direction while you shoot. Voilà! The portrait will come to life.

5. Once you have mastered this technique, you can try it in more candid situations, such as when photographing wildlife. You won't often be able to direct an animal's eyes, but, with patience, you may be lucky enough to catch the light when the animal looks in exactly the right spot.

📷 **EXPERT TIP**

A catch light is a light source that causes a bright spot of light to appear in a person's eye. It's caused by white light reflecting off the cornea. Don't confuse it with the dreaded red-eye effect, which is caused by the reflection of light from the retina inside the eye, at the back of the eyeball.

—Annie Griffiths

BACKGROUNDS

WHILE SOME BACKGROUNDS CAN BE PROBLEMATIC—especially those that contain objects that distract the viewer from the subject—others can be very useful. They can provide information to help explain what's happening in a photo or contrast to help a subject stand out. Read on to learn more.

Telling a Story

Backgrounds can be an effective storytelling tool. For example: Suppose you've taken a photo of your kid brother with a mischievous grin on his face. While his expression makes it a fun photo, it would probably be more telling if you took a step back and captured the empty cookie jar behind him. In this situation, the cookie jar provides context, or information that helps explain what's going on in a photo. Your viewers will appreciate the extra information and so will you; it will help you remember the moment when you look at the photo after many weeks, months, and even years.

📷 EXPERT TIP

The background of your photo can be your best friend or your worst enemy. If the background stays in the background, it can be a wonderful scene within which a moment takes place. If the background is full of distracting elements, your job is to get rid of it by changing your angle or throwing it out of focus with a narrow depth of field or moving to a different location. —Annie Griffiths

Creating Contrast

A close-up of a bright pink flower is nice, but it's far more powerful when set against a leafy green background. The same holds true for any object placed against a contrasting background. As you read earlier, contrast refers to the difference between two colors that appear side by side. In general, the greater the color contrast between your subject and its background, the more the subject will stand out.

Color Wheel

If you're struggling with identifying contrast colors, you might want to check out a color wheel for help. A color wheel is basically a circle with different colored sections that is used to show the relationship between colors (see page 87). Colors in the same family appear next to each other, while contrasting colors appear opposite each other in the wheel. For example, pink and green are contrasting because they appear opposite each other.

117

OFF CENTER: RULE OF THIRDS

PLACING YOUR SUBJECT IN THE CENTER OF A FRAME isn't always the best option. One reason is that everyone does it, so it can seem boring. Also, it isn't very pleasing to the eye. Instead, try moving the subject slightly off center. This will help lead the viewer into the picture and make the subject seem less boxed in. This concept is the driving force behind one of the most important rules of photography: the rule of thirds.

WHAT YOU SHOULD KNOW

To understand how the rule of thirds works, you'll have to imagine a tic-tac-toe grid drawn over a photo. When the strongest elements in the picture fall along the lines, or at the intersecting points of the grid, it creates a more pleasing photo. Keep these things in mind:

- **The Ideal Points** When taking a portrait of a person, position him or her along one of the connecting points of the grid. In scenics, the horizon is the strongest horizontal line, so try to place it high or low—not in the center!

- **Eye Contact** Human or animal subjects staring directly at the camera can make a bold, direct photo. But beautiful portraits can be made with the subject looking in other directions—especially if they are looking toward the light source.

- **Space Case** If a lot of empty space appears in the frame, experiment with adding an object or leaving it empty. Empty space can be very satisfying.

With a friend or family member as a model, try capturing different poses using the rule of thirds and then edit them to make three to five cool portraits that each feature a different take on the rule of thirds.

Supply List

- a camera
- a model
- a computer
- a clear plastic binder sleeve
- a dark felt-tip marker with a fine point
- a ruler
- a printer

STEPS

1. Photograph your model in different situations. Some photos can be only head shots, with the person looking away from the camera. Others can be full-body shots, from serious or funny poses to jumping jacks.

2. As you take each shot, imagine the tic-tac-toe grid and make sure your subject is positioned at one of the line intersections.

3. Try different backgrounds: some with empty space, some with a single prominent feature, others with several features.

4. When you've shot enough to give you a fun and lively variety, download your images to your computer and pull them up on your screen to view.

5. With a felt-tip marker, draw a tic-tac-toe grid on a plastic sleeve. Make sure the lines extend from one end of the sleeve to the other. Use a ruler to ensure that the lines are spaced evenly apart.

6. Now edit your pictures using the grid: Place it over one image. Does the subject of the photo appear along one of the intersecting points of the grid?

7. Choose the best photos and move them to a separate folder.

8. From that folder make your final selection of three to five images.

9. Print them out and frame them for a unique gift.

📷 EXPERT TIP

All rules can be broken, and that is especially true of creative rules. The rule of thirds is merely a guideline to help us understand what is usually most appealing. But don't be afraid to shake off the rules and do your own thing. I do!

—Annie Griffiths

VERTICAL OR HORIZONTAL?

LIKE CAMERAS, HUMANS VIEW THE WORLD HORIZONTALLY. That's because we have eyes that are positioned side by side. But unlike cameras, humans have peripheral vision, which allows us to see objects that are slightly to the side of, as well as above and below, our direct line of vision. So we can see tall trees and buildings, even though we have to tilt our heads back a bit to get the whole view. In order for a camera to capture such an object, you'd have to turn it vertically to the side. But vertical photos aren't just used to capture tall objects. They have other uses as well. The same applies to horizontal photos.

▶ VERTICAL SHOTS

Vertical orientation, or position, can be used for many purposes. Here are a few:

- As noted above, holding your camera vertically is a great way to capture objects that are taller than they are wide. This includes trees, buildings, balloons, doorways, windows, and more.

- Vertical orientation can also help you crop out clutter from a photograph so that the focus is on your subject.

- It's also the ideal orientation for a subject that's moving up and down, such as a bouncing ball or a person jumping on a trampoline.

📷 EXPERT TIP

A landscape photograph's strongest graphic element is often the horizon. Making a vertical composition using the horizon is harder. To get a photo on *National Geographic*'s cover you'll need to practice that!
—Annie Griffiths

▶ HORIZONTAL SHOTS

Horizontal orientation, or position, can also be used for many purposes. Here are a few:

- Horizontal orientation is ideal for capturing objects that are longer or wider than they are tall—such as a seesaw, a school bus, or a pet gecko.

- Horizontal formats work well with objects that are moving side to side. This can include a bird or a plane taking off, a kitten scampering across the floor, or a person skating across ice.

- Horizontal photos are a great way to convey the largeness of a vast space, such as a grassy meadow, a mountain range, or a football field.

THE SECRET
TO STORYTELLING

LAYERING

SOMETIMES THE MOST CAPTIVATING PHOTOS contain many different elements. When you look at these types of photos, your eye drifts from objects in the foreground (the front) to those in the background. Each item leads you through the photo and reveals something about the subject. This technique is called layering.

📷 EXPERT TIP

I don't just look at the thing itself or at the reality itself; I look around the edges for those little askew moments ... kind of like what makes up our lives ... those slightly awkward, lovely moments.
—Keith Carter, photographer

HOT SHOT: Reza

If a story touches me, I take a picture. I was exhausted from traveling in Afghanistan, and these children imitated me, playing photographer. Their laughter erased all my discouragement. A photographer's heart should be touched, because photography is nothing without emotion.

WHAT YOU SHOULD KNOW

Layering is a method in which different elements of a photo—the foreground, the subject, and the background—work together to tell a story. Using layering in your photos can be a little tricky at times. Here's what you should know:

- **Complement Your Subject** For layering to work, the elements in the foreground and background need to complement or reveal something about your subject. For example, let's say the subject of your photo is a dog with a guilty look on its face. An effective use of layering might be to have a chewed-up shoe in the foreground and your mom in the background with a disapproving look on her face.

- **Nonmoving Objects** Layering isn't so difficult when you are taking pictures of objects and landscapes. In such cases, you can either arrange the elements yourself or move to a different location to capture a good arrangement.

- **People and Animals** Layering is more difficult when you're taking candid photos of people and animals. That's because they are often moving and unpredictable. In this case, you'll need to be patient and wait for the elements to arrange themselves before you take the shot.

123

CAPTURiNG DETAiLS

TEXTURES, CURVES, AND PATTERNS

LOOK AROUND YOU. WHAT DETAILS DO YOU SEE? Experienced photographers are always on the lookout for textures, curves, and patterns in their surroundings because they know how much interest these details can add to a photo. Now let's look at how you can use these elements to your advantage as well.

Textures

You might not think twice about an object like a golf ball, but when you look at a sharp close-up of it in a photograph, the ball's dimpled texture will likely make you pause. The same applies to the spines of a cactus or the barbs of a feather. Texture is a subtle way to capture a viewer's attention. So keep an eye out for objects with unique surfaces—and remember to use lighting and shadows to accentuate them: Direct overhead lighting will cast shorter shadows, while side lighting will cast longer shadows.

Curves

Curves are another way to capture a viewer's interest. Generally, there are two types of curves: leading curves and non-leading curves. Leading curves lead a viewer's eye to a center of interest. Think of a photo that shows a person peering down from the top of a spiral staircase. Non-leading curves do not lead the viewer to a center of interest. Instead, their purpose is to provide information about the subject or to create a mood. Think of the lines created by sedimentary layers of a canyon. These lines don't have a center of interest, but rather reveal information about the canyon's makeup and how it may have been formed.

WHAT WENT WRONG?

This photo of a grassy field seems a little dull. What went wrong? And what would you do to make the image more interesting?

📷 EXPERT TIP

Be on the lookout for abstract patterns in landscapes, and then choose your lighting and viewpoint carefully. Low light, and especially side light at sundown, shows texture. A downward camera angle gets rid of the horizon. Also, try breaking up a pattern with an irregular shape or color—like one different colored tree trunk among others.

—Scott Stuckey,
National Geographic Complete Photography

MYSH📷T User: CB_oceanlover

"When it comes to details, we don't need to see how many jars are on the table or what room they're in." says NG Kids photo editor Kelley Miller.

"This photographer did a great job of zooming in on the flames and jars, while cropping out anything unrelated.

"The candlelight is also emphasized by using a shallow depth of field. The foreground is sharp and the background is out of focus. Your eye goes straight to the details of the ridges of the jar and its flickering light."

Patterns

Patterns are another great way to attract attention to a subject. However, a single pattern alone may seem a bit boring. Instead, look for objects with multiple patterns. For example, the center of a daisy is a great complement to the flower's petals. Another option might be to break up the pattern with an object. Try photographing a person lying in a field of flowers or against a stack of hay or try capturing natural objects such as a rock in a field of clovers or a log in a grassy field.

ANNIE'S ASSIGNMENT

LET PATTERNS LEAD YOUR COMPOSITION

ONE OF THE MOST IMPORTANT ELEMENTS of composition is geometry. The photographer's job is to isolate patterns and graphic lines that lead us through the image. Let's begin by looking for patterns.

ZEBRAS AT A WATER HOLE IN AFRICA'S ETOSHA NATIONAL PARK

FUN FACT

Many patterns in nature can be seen when you look at shadows! Take a walk on a sunny day and find sun patterns to photograph.

STEPS

1. Start with nature and look for simple patterns of grasses, branches, and flowers. The key is to isolate something out of a complicated scene and make it your vision. Watch for the personality of a little group of flowers or a lonely leaf hanging from a branch.

2. Next, compose your shot so that nothing will distract from the pattern in your picture. Crop those distracting elements out as you compose in the camera, not later on your computer. With digital photography it is easy to be sloppy and plan to crop everything later in an editing program. But the results are never as good as when you take the time to choose your composition carefully.

3. A telephoto lens will compress any pattern, making the graphic elements look closer together. Try composing the picture at different telephoto lengths and you will see the difference.

4. Once you get the hang of composing patterns in nature, start looking for patterns and graphic elements in every scene. You are now a pattern master!

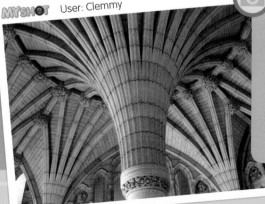

MYSHOT User: Clemmy

📷 EXPERT TIP

Photography relies on the same compositional rules as all visual arts. Geometric shapes, such as triangles, curves, and leading lines attract our eyes and help visually organize a composition. You can become a better photographer by watching for those elements in paintings, sculpture, and even dance! —Annie Griffiths

POiNT OF ViEW

FROM WHAT ANGLE DO YOU PLAN TO TAKE YOUR PHOTO? Will you look down at your subject? Or look up? Maybe you want to shoot from eye level. Whatever angle you choose, your **point of view** will have an effect on how your viewers see and interpret the image.

point of view:
the position from which your camera sees the scene

Eye Level

Think about it: When you're talking with your grandmother or best friend, you feel a deeper connection when you're sitting across from each other than you do when one person is sitting and the other is standing. The same holds true in photography. When you take a photo of a subject at eye level, you allow the viewer to feel an emotional connection to the subject.

Aiming Upward

If you ever watch a movie scene in which an ordinary person is about to do something very brave, you might notice that the camera is looking up at that character. This angle makes the subject appear greater and more powerful than he or she really is. You can use the same idea when you take pictures. When you point your camera up at a subject, you tell the viewer a subject is either great, powerful, daring, or even intimidating.

Shooting Downward

Pointing your camera down at a subject has the opposite effect of aiming upward. It makes the subject seem smaller and more inferior to the viewer. This angle works great if you're trying to draw attention to how small something is compared to its surroundings, or to emphasize how small—in a figurative sense—your subject feels after a guilty act.

Become the Subject

Another interesting way to take a photo is from the perspective of the subject. In other words, you become the subject. For example, snapping a still photo of your toes in the sand or of your doctor setting a cast on your broken arm, or getting a GoPro video of your bike adventure. When you take a photo from this perspective, your viewer will feel as if he or she is experiencing the moment firsthand.

📷 EXPERT TIP

One of the important rules of photography is to keep moving! Sometimes a very simple thing can feel new when it's shot from a different point of view. The world looks different from the point of view of an ant or from the top of a tree. This is especially true with children and pets, and it helps us understand the world they live in. So get moving! —Annie Griffiths

MAKE YOUR
SUBJECT RULE

When you look at a picture, you might think, Wow, look at that streak of lightning! Or, Aunt Meg's birthday cake looks delicious! Whatever runs through your mind is a response to the main topic, or subject, of a photo. Whether it's an animal, person, landscape, or event, all good photographs have a subject. In this section, we'll not only explore a few subjects, but we'll also show you how to make them rule!

PORTRAYING ANIMALS

JUST AS YOU'RE ABOUT TO SNAP A PHOTO OF FIDO rushing excitedly toward you, he turns away—distracted by something he hears in the distance. And no matter how loudly you call for him to return, he just won't listen. Does this sound familiar? Animals—whether they're pets or wildlife—are often unpredictable. So, how can you photograph them? Read on to learn how to tackle this challenge and more.

I want to take a close-up of my cat, but he won't stand still for a photo.

Solution: To get a close-up, eye-level shot of your pet, you'll have to crouch down or lie on the floor. But do this when your pet is least likely to be distracted, such as when it's eating. Also there are a few things your pet does that are routine: Does your cat enjoy perching on a bookshelf? Does your dog like to sleep at the foot of the bed? Think about these routines and use them to help you prepare your shots ahead of time.

I hope to take photos of the wildlife in my backyard, but I don't know where to look.

Solution: Do your research. Figure out where in your backyard you're most likely to see these critters. Bright-colored flowers attract bees and hummingbirds, while an acorn tree is a magnet for squirrels. Keep in mind that most backyard critters are shy and scurry away the second someone gets too close, so you'll have to get creative to get a shot. Consider hiding beneath a sheet or blanket, but make sure your camera lens isn't covered. Also, since these animals move quickly, you'll need to do the same. If you can, use a fast shutter speed.

I want to take pictures of the fish at the aquarium, but the glass gets in the way.

Solution: You can't avoid the aquarium glass or the bars at a zoo. But you can move in closer. To capture the most detail possible, keep the lens flush with the zoo bars or place it against the aquarium glass (this minimizes reflection, too).

My family is going on a safari adventure. I want to photograph the lions, but I know I won't be able to get close.

Solution: Lucky you! Whether you're taking photos of an animal at a zoo or on safari, you shouldn't get too close. To get a portrait, you'll need to use a telephoto lens if you have one. Remember, closer isn't always better. If you're lucky enough to be on a safari, take photos of animals in the trees and tall grasses, or having a drink at a watering hole. In a zoo, this could involve showing a zookeeper interacting with the animals or capturing crowds of people viewing the animals.

ANNIE'S ASSIGNMENT

WILDLIFE IN YOUR OWN BACKYARD

PHOTOGRAPHING WILDLIFE CAN BEGIN IN YOUR NEIGHBORHOOD, where you can practice all of the skills you will ever need. Think about all of the birds, small mammals, amphibians, and even insects that share your world ... and start shooting!

FUN FACT
The first wildlife photographs in *National Geographic* magazine were printed in 1906. The article, with pictures by George Shiras, was so popular that it was reprinted two years later!

A HUMMINGBIRD DRINKS FROM A BIRD FEEDER IN WISCONSIN.

📷 EXPERT TIP

Wildlife photography is one of the most popular specialties at National Geographic, but it is also one of the most challenging. Wildlife photographers must be technical masters, scientists, and some of the most patient people on earth. They endure extreme weather, insects, and disease—all to bring back amazing moments from the natural world.
—Annie Griffiths

4. Park yourself near a pond or small body of water where turtles and frogs hang out. As with all wildlife, move slowly and quietly to a position where you have a good view. Lie on the ground and keep your patience because it will take time before these critters reemerge from the water.

STEPS

1. Birds: Start by finding a spot where birds congregate: a feeder, a bird bath, or a berry tree. Observe the times of day when they are most active and when the light is beautiful. Birds are easily alarmed by shapes and movement, so find or create a hiding place. Shooting from a parked car or through an open window or door works well because birds know those shapes and aren't alarmed by your figure inside.

2. If you live near water, try attracting ducks, geese, and swans with bread crumbs. Practice slowly panning (following the action with your camera as you stand in one place) as they swim by.

3. Squirrels, chipmunks, and gophers are great subjects for animal behavior. See if you can get low and photograph them through grasses or leaves.

SHOT User: Fungirlpuppypop

135

CAPTURING PEOPLE

YOU PROBABLY TAKE PHOTOS OF PEOPLE more than any other subject. So snapping these shots is easy, right? Well, there's a lot more that goes into taking a great portrait or candid photo than you think.

My kid sister is funny and energetic, but she gets really uncomfortable when I try to take her picture.

Solution: Not everyone is comfortable in front of a camera. As the photographer, it's your job to help them relax. How do you do this? Think about your subject. What are his or her interests or favorite games and movies? Talk about them. The goal is to put your subjects at ease by helping them forget about the camera. Asking people to say "cheese" will result in a forced, unnatural looking smile. Just before you push the button, look up over the top and raise your eyebrows with a funny expression. The surprise is sure to bring natural smiles.

I'm having trouble taking a flattering portrait of my subject.

Solution: When you're taking a **portrait** of a person, you need to think about the lighting. Window light is always flattering on people. You may or may not want to use a flash (see page 96). Also, since the person you are photographing is the main attraction of your photo, move in close so that he or she fills the frame.

portrait:
a picture where a person is
the clear subject of the image

EXPERT TIP

It's one thing to make a picture of what a person looks like; it's another thing to make a portrait of who they are.

—Paul Caponigro, photographer

I enjoy taking pictures of people on the street, but sometimes they move too quickly for me to catch them on camera.

Solution: This is a common problem when taking candids or pictures of people who are moving around, who are often unaware of the camera. Since these subjects aren't sitting around posing for you, you have to respond quickly. To save time, make sure you know your camera controls well enough so that you don't have to fumble with them. Otherwise, consider setting your digital camera to shutter priority mode (see page 150) so that you don't have to worry about settings. Also, it may be tempting to hold the shutter button down to get a continuous burst of shots, but don't do it! The noise from your camera will likely distract your subject.

DID YOU KNOW?

WHEN THE FIRST PORTRAITS WERE TAKEN in the 19th century, people rarely smiled. Why? There are a few possible reasons. First, the exposure time was long—sometimes up to 15 minutes—so it was difficult for a person to hold a smile for such a lengthy period. Also, to have a picture taken was very expensive at the time, so a serious look seemed more appropriate. Thirdly, dental hygiene wasn't the best in 1800s, so it's possible that people didn't want to show their rotten teeth.

CAPTURING EVENTS

EVENTS SUCH AS PARTIES, GRADUATIONS, AND HOLIDAYS are joyful moments that can happen in the blink of an eye. Don't get caught off guard! Here are a few common pitfalls—and suggestions for how to avoid them.

I tried to photograph my older sister accepting her high-school diploma, but too many people were blocking my view.

Solution: When you're attending a formal event such as a graduation, a wedding, or even a birthday party, many people will be clamoring to get photos. Do your research before an event to determine where the main action will take place. Then scope out a location where you can stand to get a good shot—get there early and hang out until it happens.

All of my Thanksgiving photos show my family seated around the dinner table. The photos seem boring and I can't figure out why.

Solution: Earlier in the book, we talked about using your photos to tell a story. You do this by taking pictures of various key moments of an event. In this case, you could have photographed guests arriving, the centerpiece at the table, the turkey being carved at the table, your cousin with a mouthful of food, and so on. Got it?

📷 EXPERT TIP

When photographing an event, keep in mind that the crowd is often as interesting as the main act. Try to tell a picture story that includes an overall view, performers and crowd, and details that complete your story.
—Annie Griffiths

> I'm sitting in the upper deck of a baseball stadium. When I take photos of the players on the field, they look like tiny insects.

Solution: A standard camera lens won't help you take close shots of objects that are far away. Consider using a longer telephoto lens. Standard point-and-shoot cameras have an optical zoom lens that can move in closer. If you can't get as close as you want to, you may want to focus more on the experience of the game (the crowd reacting to a home run, the messages on the jumbo screen overlooking the field, the hot dog you're eating, etc.).

> I'm at a concert, trying to photograph my favorite band as they perform. However, all of my photos are washed out.

Solution: You'll need to underexpose your shot. Here's how it works: At concerts and other performances, bright lights stream down on the performers. Behind them, it's black. The camera meter sees all that black and compensates for it. So it overexposes the people in front who are already covered in light, making them look washed out. If you set your camera to underexpose, you'll get a photo that's just right.

CAREERS FOR CAMERA HOUNDS

WHO: Melissa Farlow

JOB: Photographer

Q What was one of your first experiences in photography?

A In high school, I tried out as a photographer for the school's sport sponsor at a baseball game. I wasn't prepared, so I blew it!

Q When did you decide to give photography another shot?

A At Indiana University I took a photojournalism class, then got a job at the *Courier-Journal* in Louisville, Kentucky.

Q What type of photos did you take for the newspaper?

A Everything from people to school sports. Louisville is home to the Kentucky Derby, so I took photos of that, too!

Q How challenging was it to take photos at the Kentucky Derby?

A Very! The horses run by you only once. Before the race I'd find a good spot and practice taking the photo again and again.

Q Do you have advice for kids who are interested in photography as a career?

A Combine your main interest— plants, animals, or cultures— with photography so you're following something.

ANNiE'S ASSiGNMENT

PHOTOGRAPHING A GROUP

WHETHER FOR A FAMILY REUNION, a sports team, or a holiday card, group pictures are often deadly dull. But they don't have to be! The best group portraits happen when the photographer loosens everyone up.

A HAPPY CARLOAD OF KIDS IN FLORIDA

📷 EXPERT TIP

Sometimes the very best group shot happens immediately after everyone thinks the shot is finished. Keep shooting, especially at occasions like a wedding, where candid moments are so wonderful. —Annie Griffiths

STEPS

1. Get your subjects to loosen up! People often look awkward because they don't know what to do with their hands. Tell classmates to throw their arms around each other or touch heads together. Ask your brother to lean on his buddy. The more you tease and cajole, the more your subjects will loosen up. You will see an immediate change in their faces as well as in their body language.

2. Tighten up the shot! We don't need to see their shoes. What we care about are their faces, so make a composition that is nice and tight around their faces whenever possible.

3. If you're taking a team picture, make it fun instead of having everyone line up like robots. Ask the coach to lie on his or her side on the ground. Then have the team all get down and lean on the coach in some way. Guaranteed smiles!

4. In large groups, remind people that if they don't have a clear view of the camera, then their face won't be clearly in the shot.

5. The best family photos show the love! Pile everyone on top of Mom and Dad or have the whole gang snuggle in a single chair. You can even have the parents lie on the ground and have the kids make a pyramid on top of them.

LOOSEN UP

TIGHTEN UP

MAKE IT FUN

SHOW THE LOVE

FUN FACT

Before the invention of photography, only wealthy families could afford to have pictures painted, so most families had no images of themselves or their ancestors. Today, when people are asked what they would take with them out of a burning building, most mention their family pictures.

SECRETS
OF THE TRADE

EXTREME WEATHER

MOST PEOPLE ARE TERRIFIED AT THE THOUGHT OF EXTREME WEATHER—but not Jim Reed. He's been taking prizewinning photographs of tornadoes, hurricanes, blizzards, and floods for more than 20 years. Jim shares some of his experiences—and secrets to taking top-notch weather photos.

Q1 **How did you get into extreme weather?**

My interest in weather has been there since I was six or seven. I was raised in Illinois, where there are many types of extreme weather—ice storms, tornadoes, blizzards, floods. And that caught my interest. But it wasn't until I was a student at the University of Southern California that I decided to combine weather and photography. Around that time, I was working on a production that was rained on. In fact, it rained for days! That's when it occurred to me that I should point my camera to the sky. The rest is history.

Q2 **You've taken photos of many different types of weather. What's the most challenging?**

Believe it or not, rainbows! I often tell people that if you have any desire to photograph tornadoes, you should start with rainbows! That's because you need to have enough knowledge about where it's going to form—just like a tornado. Also, rainbows don't last very long so you have to be quick, which means you need to know your gear well.

Q3 Any tips on how to spot—and photograph—rainbows?

When it's raining, try to spot sunlight peering through the clouds. That's usually where rainbows form. When you do see one, think about different ways to shoot it. People often take horizontal photos of rainbows to get most of it in the frame. But I recommend zooming in on a small area of the rainbow and taking a vertical shot of it. Its bright colors will really pop against the dark sky.

Q4 When I try to capture rain or wind on camera, it never really shows. Is there anything I can do?

When photographing rain or wind you need to have some context. For rain, you might want to have someone with an umbrella in the photo or even a car windshield. With wind, try to find something that's being moved by the wind—such as clothing on a clothesline or the swings of a swing set. With wind, you want to illustrate motion.

Q5 Is it ever a good idea to photograph lightning?

You shouldn't be outside if there's lightning, so unless you have a remote (see page 93), don't do it! Lightning is very unpredictable—and very risky.

Q6 I love snow! Is there a good time to photograph it?

Yes. Try to snap photos right after the storm has ended. At this point, no one has begun shoveling and everything is still covered by it. Also, pay attention to the sky. If the clouds have parted and the sky is blue, the snow will also have a blue tint because it's reflective. The only way to correct that will be by using a filter on your camera or tweaking it with photo-editing software.

Q7 What advice do you have for budding weather photographers?

Learn about your subject. The more you know about the type of weather you're photographing, the safer you'll be. If you're really serious about it, look into the free "spotter talks" sponsored by the National Weather Service. These talks are given at the organization's local offices and usually take place before storm season. You'll not only learn a lot about the topic, but you'll meet many people who'll give you some great tips.

SHOOTING LANDSCAPES

WHETHER IT'S THE ROCK FORMATIONS OF THE GRAND CANYON or the prairies of the Great Plains, landscapes can be very dramatic. In fact, many amateur photographers get so caught up in the beauty of these surroundings that they forget to think like a photographer. As a result, the photos end up dull. What are some challenges landscape photographers face?

I'm not sure what I should be photographing.

Solution: You can start by looking for some interesting elements that will draw the viewer in, such as a winding road, the angle of a cliff, or sunlight streaming through the trees of a forest. Otherwise, try to convey a mood. Ask yourself, what adjectives would I use to describe this place? Flat, open land may strike you as lonely, so you might photograph a farmhouse or a prairie dog gazing in the distance. Or, if you're in a desert, the heat may strike you as severe. To convey this mood you could photograph a lone cactus or a tall sand dune.

There's so much to see, but I can't capture it all in one frame.

Solution: To capture a huge sweeping shot of a landscape, try a wide-angle lens with a focal point that is less than 55 mm. Many smartphone cameras have a panoramic feature that will allow you to capture a wider view of your surroundings.

I think the sky looks cool against the landscape, but I don't know how much of it to include in the frame.

Solution: The sky—especially when it's filled with billowy clouds—can add a lot of interest to a photo. If the sky is beautiful, let it fill most of the frame by keeping the horizon low. If the sky is dull, put that horizon up high!

SMARTPHONE PROJECTOR & SHOW!

It's fun to flip through your images on your phone or computer screen, but it's even better to get the full impact of projecting them onto a big surface.

Supply List

- black spray paint
- a shoe box
- a magnifying glass
- a pencil
- an X-Acto knife
- black duct tape
- a large paper clip
- a smartphone
- a white bedsheet for a screen

STEPS

1. Spray-paint the inside of the shoe box black so its dark for projection.

2. When the box is dry, hold the magnifying glass to one short end and trace around it with a pencil.

3. Ask an adult to help you use the X-Acto knife to cut out the circle you traced.

4. Place the magnifying glass over the circular hole and duct-tape it securely to the box, closing any gaps.

5. Bend the paper clip into a stand for your smartphone. Several websites give instructions for making a stand out of a paper clip.

6. Set your phone so that the image will appear upside down on the screen. (The image will flip to right side up as it goes through the magnifying glass.)

7. Turn the phone screen brightness all the way up; turn the room lights down.

8. Set your phone (with upside-down photos on the screen) on the paper clip stand near the back of the box, opposite the magnifying glass.

9. Hang the bedsheet along a wall or over a doorway.

10. Hold the box with the magnifying glass pointing forward and walk toward the screen until the image is in focus; set the projector down on a stool.

11. To keep your phone powered, poke a small hole in the back of the box and feed through the phone cord.

EXPERT TIP

Landscapes generally should not look far away. Include foreground elements in your picture, so that the viewer is more likely to feel he is standing right there with you. My go-to lens for scenics is always a wide angle.
—Annie Griffiths

CAPTURiNG TRAVEL

WHETHER YOU'RE VISITING A DESTINATION that's a few miles from home or one that's halfway around the world, consider yourself lucky! New surroundings are terrific subjects for photographs. Here's what you should know to make the best of every travel-photo opportunity.

I took photos of all the famous monuments, but none of my friends seem too excited about them.

Solution: There's nothing wrong with taking photos of famous monuments, but if you find that your viewers aren't too enthused, it's probably because they've seen hundreds of photos of those same subjects in postcards, books, and magazines. For a better response, try to capture any action happening around the monuments. For example, snap a street performer or a double-decker bus driving past Big Ben. Or, try to photograph the monuments from interesting angles or when they're lit up at night. Floodlights used to light up monuments can look beautiful against night skies.

Aside from the famous landmarks, I don't know what I should be photographing.

Solution: Wherever your trip takes you, you'll want to capture your personal experience of the adventure. For example, you might show local markets you visited, food you ate, or even signs printed in other languages if you visited a foreign country. Also, take candid photos of your relatives interacting with the environment. For example, snap a photo of your mom looking at antiques or souvenirs, your dad asking a local person for directions, or your brother buried neck-deep in the sand. And if they do insist on posing, have them do something funny, like pretending to hold up the Leaning Tower of Pisa!

EXPERT TIP

Travel photographers are often in places where hundreds of people are taking pictures. The local people can build up resentment. There is only one solution: Spend time with people or don't take the picture. Photographers must earn their photographs through hard work and an investment of time. If a picture is worth getting, it is worth spending time with someone to get it.

—Annie Griffiths

I'm visiting a city with many skyscrapers. The streets are so crowded that when I try to take photos of the buildings, my view is blocked.

Solution: In large cities it can be a challenge to get an unblocked view of a building, but it's not impossible. One option is to photograph the skyline. To do this, you'll need to find a place with a good view. Look at tourist brochures or ask locals for recommendations. Another option is to move in close and aim your camera up toward the top of the building. You may also want to take close-ups of any details, such as intricate ironwork, unusual carvings—such as gargoyles—or reflections in a glass façade.

ANNIE'S ASSIGNMENT

TURN YOUR VACATION INTO A PICTURE STORY

IF YOU LOVE PHOTOGRAPHY, TELLING A STORY with pictures is one way to keep you creative on a vacation. A travel story should make people feel like they are traveling along in your camera bag. Take only the gear you need: Too much weighs you down and draws unwanted attention. Also, get to know the locals!

THIS CLOSE-UP OF FLIPPERS BRINGS EXTRA COLOR TO THE LOCAL BACKGROUND.

FUN FACT

National Geographic photographers always research their travel destination and its customs. Besides finding the best places and situations to shoot, they learn when it's okay to take a photo, and when it's not.

5. Make a friend. If you see someone whom you would like to photograph, don't sneak a picture from across the street. Of course, be smart and safe when talking to strangers, but do ask. The best pictures are earned when you spend a little time with your subject.

6. Turn your story into an online book. You're the editor, so remember to include only the best images. One great shot of the sunset is better than five! Sequence your pictures to tell your story the best way possible. Remember to have a great cover and a fun ending!

STEPS

1. Have a plan. Research the place you are going to learn about events and activities that are happening during the time you will be there.

2. Think about a story line that gives your vacation photos meaning. For example, feature one member of your family and tell the story from his or her point of view, or arrange to spend time with a local person whom you have learned about.

3. Remember that any story needs to have a variety of shots: scene setters, details, portraits, and wonderful moments.

4. Don't be too literal. It's much more fun to see a colorfully dressed couple or a kid eating ice cream in front of a monument than it is to see just the monument. It's better to show a dog jumping into a lake than to show only the lake.

MYSHOT   User: Katnissmockingjay

📷 EXPERT TIP

Remember that most people are flattered if you ask to take their picture or spend time with them. It makes them feel special. Think about how much fun it would be if you or a friend appeared in the newspaper or on TV! —Annie Griffiths

EQUIPMENT SETTINGS

ISO AND MODES

THE MORE YOU PHOTOGRAPH the more you'll become familiar with the settings on your camera and when to use them. Your manual will guide you—along with these basic terms:

ISO You can adjust the ISO setting on both film and digital cameras. ISO ranges from 25 to as high as 25,600. The higher the rating, the more light sensitive the film or digital sensor. In low light use a high ISO, such as 1600. In bright light, use a low ISO, such as 100.

Modes On page 21, the mode dial on the camera also has manual and automatic settings such as the ones below. Check your manual to see which ones you have.

    Automatic mode: For beginners, it tells the camera to make its best judgment to select shutter speed, aperture, ISO, etc. Below are additional auto settings for specific situations.

    Portrait mode: selects a large aperture (small number), putting your subject in focus and your background out of focus (shallow depth of field)

    Macro mode: allows you to use a regular lens to get a close-up of small objects like flowers or bugs

    Landscape mode: selects a small aperture (large number), which puts big areas—not just one subject—in focus (deep depth of field)

    Sports mode: freezes fast-moving action by increasing the shutter speed

    Night mode: selects a long shutter speed to capture images in the dark and has a flash to light the subject in the foreground

    Movie mode: records both video and sound

    AWB: Automatic white balance lets your camera read color temperatures to give you the truest color under different lights. To refine AWB, you can use settings for specific lighting situations, including fluorescent and tungsten.

M: In manual mode, you make all the adjustments to aperture, shutter speed, ISO, etc., for each situation. Beginners: Use the automatic mode and try these priority modes to refine your shots.

Priority Modes These manual settings help you refine an automatic shot, so you have some control over the decisions it makes:

    A or AV: Aperture mode. You choose the aperture and then your camera selects the shutter speed. A large number aperture will let in less light, so your camera will automatically choose a slower shutter speed. If you use a small number aperture, letting in more light, your camera will choose a fast shutter speed.

    S or TV: Shutter priority. You select a shutter speed, and then the camera chooses the aperture. For instance, a fast shutter speed captures action; a slow shutter speed is good in low light or for blurring.

    B: Bulb setting. This allows you to shoot in low light by keeping the shutter open for as long as you depress the shutter button. See Annie's Assignment, page 92.

    P: Program mode. Like automatic mode, this sets the shutter speed and aperture, but it allows more control over functions such as flash, white balance, etc. Your camera manual has specifics.

    C 1, 2, 3: These are custom modes. You can program these so the settings are always the same for a certain kind of shot. Check your camera manual for more.

1. **Be prepared.** Few things are worse than missing a great shot because you weren't ready. Do your homework: Familiarize yourself with your camera's functions before you start shooting so that you don't have to think too much about it. Also, keep the shutter button pressed halfway down just before taking a photo to avoid shutter lag. Then press it down completely when you're ready for the shot.

2. **Pay attention to what is attracting your eye—and be selective.** Before pressing that shutter button, ask yourself: What are the strongest elements here? Then try to eliminate anything that distracts from your main subject. It's better to take a few well-thought-out photos than to shoot like a maniac!

3. **Move in—especially when you photograph people.** Remember, it's the face of a person that we connect with. Focus on an expression or a beautiful silhouette. Even showing part of a face, such as sparkling eyes or a joyful smile, can tell a story and make an unforgettable photograph.

4. **Keep it steady.** Blurry photos are often the result of camera shake, which occurs when your shutter speed is too slow for you to hold the camera steady. To make yourself steadier, use your left hand to cradle the bottom of the camera and your right hand to grip the side. In addition, hold the camera close to your body, keeping your elbows tight against your torso.

5. **Limit your use of flash.** Most amateur photographers use flash more often than they should. As a result, they forget to take advantage of softer light that is in the room. Flash should be used only if it is too dark for you to shoot without blurriness. But if that isn't the case, opt for natural light streaming through a window, or artificial lighting from lamps and ceiling lights.

6. **Think about the most flattering light when you photograph people.** Avoid photographing people or objects in direct sunlight, which is harsh and unflattering. An overcast day is actually much nicer for photography. Indoors, overhead lighting creates shorter shadows, while side lighting creates long, deep shadows.

7. **Think about your composition—and MOVE to make it happen.** The way the elements in a photo are arranged can make a difference between a photo that's interesting and one that isn't. Avoid busy backgrounds—move around your subject to find the best setting and to make sure the different objects in your photo relate to the subject. Also, follow the rule of thirds: Usually you won't want your subject directly in the center of the photograph.

8. **Use your camera's highest quality setting.** Save the files in JPEGs between 8 MB and 12 MB for high quality that doesn't take up too much memory on your computer—storage overload can be a huge problem! Pros shoot in super-high-quality raw format, but you'll be fine with the highest quality JPEGs your camera makes.

9. **Organize your photos with relevant file names.** Finding a specific photo is a lot easier when it's labeled "Summer Camp" along with or instead of "IMG_61524.jpg." So rename your digital files after you upload them to your computer hard drive. It will also prevent photos from having the same name.

10. **Look at pro photos and learn from them.** Think about how the photographer composed the picture, the quality of light, and what emotion the photo elicits, and then try your own! Mostly, have fun!

GLOSSARY

aperture an opening inside a lens that controls the amount of light that enters a camera. A large aperture lets in more light, while a small aperture lets in less light.

autofocus a system in a digital camera that enables it to automatically focus on the main subject.

bokeh (BOH-kay) the artistic blur in the out-of-focus parts of an image. It is produced by the lens.

candid photo photo of one or more persons who are often unaware that a photo is being taken.

composition the arrangement of every-thing in your picture. This includes the subject, foreground, background, and surrounding elements.

depth of field the range of focus of a photograph. A photograph with a wide depth of field is sharp everywhere. A photograph with a shallow depth of field is focused in only a small area.

exposure the amount of light coming into a camera and the length of time it strikes the sensor or film.

f-stop the number on a camera that indicates the size of the aperture. A lower f-stop number increases the size of the aperture; a higher f-stop number decreases it.

focal length the distance from the center of a lens to the sensor or film.

golden hour the time just after sunrise or before sunset when daylight is softer and redder than in midday.

hue the properties of a color, or a shade of color.

ISO rating this number indicates the light sensitivity of your digital sensor or your film. Ratings range from ISO 25 (for bright conditions) to as high as 25,600 (for dim conditions).

layering a method in which elements of a photo work together to tell a story. Elements can include the foreground, subject, and background.

lens the glass in front of a camera that gathers light, focuses it, and directs it into the camera and onto the sensor.

lens flare In bright midday sun, stray light can reflect instead of refract (as it should) inside of the lens. This can look artistic—as though it's hot outside; or it can look like a foggy mistake.

light-capturing system the part of a camera where light rays converge. In a film camera, the light-capturing system is film. In a digital camera, the light-capturing system is a sensor.

liquid crystal display (LCD) the screen on the back of a digital camera that allows a photographer to view a photograph immediately after it is taken.

JPEG (aka JPG) a file format for digital photos that is recognized by most computer software and contains less information than a TIFF or raw file.

JPEG stands for Joint Photographic Experts Group.

macro lens used for extreme close-ups. It brings small objects into focus from a supershort distance and makes them large enough to fill the frame.

noise when you photograph in low light with a high ISO, specks of color can show up, making the photo appear grainy, unclear, or distorted.

pixel the smallest bit of information in a digital image. Multiple pixels combine to form a digital photograph. The word "pixel" is an abbreviation of picture (pix) and element (el).

point of view the position from which your camera sees a particular scene.

portrait a photo taken of a person or animal, often a pet.

raw a digital photo format that has not been altered in any way.

resolution the number of pixels that make up a digital photograph. A high-resolution photograph has many pixels, while a low-resolution photograph has fewer pixels.

rule of thirds the practice of placing the main subject off center in a composition, where imaginary tic-tac-toe grid lines intersect.

sensor an object behind the digital camera lens that converts incoming light rays into electronic signals.

shutter a shade located in front of the sensor or film of a camera that opens when the shutter button is pressed. When the shutter opens, light rays strike the sensor or film.

shutter button the button on a camera that a photographer presses to take a picture.

subject the main topic of a photograph.

telephoto lens a lens that has a longer focal length than a standard lens (greater than 55 mm), which makes distant objects look closer.

TIFF a file format for digital photos that contains information about a photo and is recognized by most computer software. TIFF stands for Tagged Image File Format.

tripod a three-legged stand used to support a camera.

viewfinder a small window on a camera that a photographer looks through to see the subject.

white balance a camera setting that allows the photographer to adjust the color of light in an image.

wide-angle lens a lens that has a shorter focal length (less than 55 mm) than a standard lens and captures more of the area surrounding a subject.

zoom a lens that has an adjustable angle of view (shorter to longer and longer to shorter).

EQUIPMENT
BASICS

WHETHER YOU'RE TRAVELING TO ANOTHER COUNTRY or simply going on a hike near your home, you'll need to keep camera equipment in mind. Here are a few things to remember:

Carrying case Keep it light. There's no need to carry a large, clunky camera bag when traveling. Look for a compact bag with foam padding that will protect your equipment and keep it from bouncing around. The bag should also be made from a tough, water-resistant material to withstand rain and other precipitation, and it should have strong seams that won't come apart easily.

Cleaning equipment You've learned in this book that a cotton ball dabbed in rubbing alcohol is a great tool to clean your camera lens. But let's face it: Rubbing alcohol isn't the easiest item to carry when you're traveling. When you're on the go, opt for packets of lens wipes or a lens pen instead.

Memory card Digital cameras have only a limited amount of memory for storing photos, so remember to take a memory card. Memory cards come in different sizes. If you shoot mainly photos, a 1 gigabyte (GB) card for photos should work well. But if you take a lot of videos, you'll want a chip that holds a lot more memory, such as 4 GB.

Underwater housing If you're into snorkeling or scuba diving and want to bring your camera along, consider buying underwater housing. This waterproof case is designed to protect your camera during dives and is available at most camera stores. Be sure to test your housing thoroughly before placing your camera inside. You'll want to make sure that it seals properly and that there are no leaks.

Tripod If you need to keep your camera steady for extended periods of time, consider taking a small, lightweight tripod—GorillaPod is an affordable alternative with flexible legs that can bend around a pole or fence. This nifty stand will prop up the camera for you so that you can take pictures without having to worry about camera shake.

RESOURCES

BOOKS

Burian, Peter K., and Robert Caputo. *National Geographic Photography Field Guide.* 2nd ed. Washington, DC: National Geographic Society, 2003.

Cope, Peter. *100 Ways to Make Good Photos Great.* Blue Ash, OH: David & Charles-F&W Media International, Ltd., 2013.

Gerlach, John, and Barbara Gerlach. *Digital Nature Photography: The Art and Science.* Jordan Hill, Oxford, UK: Focal Press-Elsevier, 2012.

Gernsheim, Helmut. *A Concise History of Photography.* Toronto, Ontario: General Publishing Company, Ltd., 1986.

Hirsch, Robert, and John Valentino. *Photographic Possibilities.* 2nd ed. Woburn, MA: Focal Press, 2001.

Hurter, Bill. *Children's Portrait Photography Handbook.* Buffalo, NY: Amherst Media, 2010.

Johnson, Daniel. *4-H Guide to Digital Photography.* Minneapolis, MN: Voyageur Press, 2009.

Johnson, Neil. *National Geographic Photography Guide for Kids.* Washington, DC: National Geographic Society, 2001.

Krages, Bert. *Photography: The Art of Composition.* New York: Allworth Press, 2005.

Krist, Bob. *Digital Masters: Travel Photography: Documenting the World's People and Places.* Toronto, Ontario: Lark Books, 2008.

Long, Ben. *Complete Digital Photography.* 7th ed. Boston: Course Technology-Cengage Learning, 2012.

Moschovi, Alexandra, Carol McKay, and Arabella Plouviez, eds. *The Versatile Image: Photography, Digital Technologies, and the Internet.* Belgium: Leuven University Press, 2013.

Sartore, Joel, with John Healey. *Photographing Your Family.* Washington, DC: National Geographic Society, 2008.

WEBSITES

Be sure you go online with a parent or adult.

cambridgeincolour.com

canon.com

digitalcameraworld.com

eastmanhouse.org

kodak.com

metmuseum.org

nikonusa.com

photography.nationalgeographic.com

picmonkey.com

polaroid.com

Fully colored image from page 23

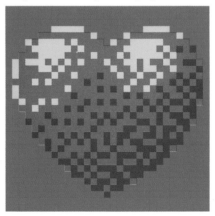

iNDEX

Boldface indicates illustrations.

A
Adams, John Quincy **10**
Animals, photography of 34–35, **132–135**
Aperture 16, 76–77, 79, 81, 150, 152
Apps 26, 75
Autofocus **74,** 74–75, **75,** 152

B
Babies, photography of 27, **27,** 34–35, **35**
Back lighting 89, **89,** 99, **99**
Backgrounds 55, **55, 116,** 116–117, **117**
Batteries 20, **20**
Black-and-white photography 26, 36
Blogging 64
Blurry photographs **44,** 44–45, **45,** 55
Body of camera 16, **16**
Bokeh 152
Brightness 55
Bytes 60

C
Camera bags 40, **40**
Camera modes 21, **21,** 150
Camera obscura 10
Camera phones **26,** 26–27, 75, 145, **145**
Camera straps 48, **48,** 49, **49**
Cameras
    care for **40,** 40–41, **41**
    how they work 16, **16**
    parts 16, **16**
    timeline 11, **11**
Candid photos **34,** 34–35, **35,** 152
Careers
    digital imaging technician 57
    macro photographer 113, **113**
    National Geographic staff
        photographer 89, **89**
    photographer 139, **139**
    special projects assistant 67
Cartier-Bresson, Henri 29
Catch light **114,** 114–115, **115**
Cell phones **26,** 26–27, 75, 145, **145**
Chiaroscuro 83, **83**
Chimping 47
Chin, Jimmy 111, **111**
Clone 58
Close-up filters 112
Close-up shots 112, **112,** 132, **132,** 151
Cloud storage 62, **62**

Color correction **56,** 56–57, **57,** 95, **95**
Color film 36
Color wheel 87, **87,** 117, **117**
Composition **46,** 46–47, **47, 106,** 106–107, **107**
    definition 12, 106, 152
    fireworks 93
    patterns **126,** 126–127, **127**
    street photography 29
    tips 12, 151
Computers, for photo storage 62, 63, **63**
Contests 66, **66–67**
Contrast 55, 117, **117**
Crafts **68,** 68–69, **69**
Cropping 55
Curves 124, **124**

D
Daylight **86,** 86–87, **87,** 103
Degas, Edgar 110
Depth of field 73, **76–79,** 152
Developing film 36
Digital cameras
    parts 20–21, **20–21**
    pixels 22–23
    resolution 22, **22**
    timeline 11, **11**
Digital zoom lenses 25
Disposable cameras 38–39, **39**
Documentaries 33, **33**
Doorway studios **50,** 50–51, **51**
Doubilet, David 31, **31**

E
Eastman, George 11, **11**
Editing
    careers 57
    color correction **56,** 56–57, **57**
    photo correction **54,** 54–55, **55**
    to tell a story **52,** 52–53, **53**
Edwards, Neal 57, **57**
Epstein, Lori **52,** 52–53
Equipment
    basics **14–41,** 154
    carrying tips 48, **48,** 154
    cleaning 154
    settings 150
Events, photography of **138,** 138–139, **139**
Exposure 51, 80–81, 139, 152
External drives 62, **62**

F
F-stop 79, 152

Facial recognition 75
Farlow, Melissa 139, **139**
Fashion photography 51
File formats 60–61, 151
File names 63, **63**
Film, invention of 11
Film cameras 36, **36**
Film speed 36
Filters 26, 112
Fireworks **92,** 92–93, **93**
Flash **96,** 96–97, **97**
    camera settings 25, **25**
    limiting use of 151
    underwater photography 30, **31**
Flash memory 32
Flashlights 100–101
Fluorescent lights 94, **94**
Focal length 18, 19, 152
Focus, choosing **76,** 76–77, **77**
Frames 68, **68,** 110, 111
Framing **110,** 110–111, **111**
Front lighting 88, **88**

G
Glossary 152–153
Goertzel, Laura 8
Golden hour 86, 152
Griffiths, Annie 6, **6**
Groups, photography of **140,** 140–141, **141**

H
Halogen lights 94, **94**
Hard light 82, **82**
Harrison, William Henry 10
HDR (high dynamic range) imaging 26, 27, **27**
High-resolution images 22
Horizontal shots 120–121, **121**
Hue 152
Human eye **72,** 72–73

I
Image stabilization 45
Incandescent light 94, **94**
Indoor lighting 94, **94,** 94–95, **95,** 103
Internet safety 64
ISO rating 36, 39, 150, 152

J
JPEG 60, 152–153

K
Kahn, Phillippe 27

L

Land, Edwin 11
Landscapes 18, **18**, 144, **144**, 150
Layering **122**, 122–123, **123**, 152
LCD screens 20, **20**, 25, 32, 152
Lens caps 41, **41**
Lens flare 152
Lens hoods 41, **41**
Lenses
    care for 40, **40**, 41, **41**
    close-up shots 112
    definition 152
    function 16, **16**
    types 18, **18**
    vs. human eye **72**, 72–73, **73**
Library of Congress, Washington,
    D.C. 63, **63**
Light-capturing system 16, 152
Light quality **82–87**
Lighting
    back lighting 89, **89**, 99, **99**
    challenges 102–103
    directions **88**, 88–89, **89**
    front lighting 88, **88**
    indoor **94**, 94–95, **95**
    portraits 136, **136**, 151
    selfies 65
    tips 151
Liquid crystal display (LCD) 20, **20**,
    25, 32, 152
Long exposures 84, **92**, 92–93, **93**
Low-resolution images 22
Lumière brothers 11

M

Macro lenses 112, 153
Macro photography 113, **113**, 150
McGrory, Marie 129, 137
Memory cards 20, **20**, 32, **32**, 154
Miller, Kelley **52**, 52–53, 95, 99, 125,
    133
Motion photography 11, **11**
Mozi (Chinese philosopher) 10
Murawski, Darlyne 113, **113**
Muybridge, Eadweard 11
My Shot 8, **8**, 66, **66–67**, 67, **67**

N

Niépce, Nicéphore 10
Night photography **98–101**, 150
Noise 137, 153

O

Optical image stabilization 45
Optical zoom lenses 25, 112
Organizing photos 63, 151
Orientation **120**, 120–121, **121**

P

Patterns **125–127**
People, photography of **136**, 136–137,
    137
    camera settings 150
    candid photos **34**, 34–35,
    35, 152

catch light **114**, 114–115, **115**
doorway studios **50**, 50–51, **51**
groups **140**, 140–141, **141**
lenses 18, **18**
lighting 151
portraits 136, 153
sunlight 13
tips 12, 13
Pets, photography of 34–35, 132, **132**
Phones **26**, 26–27, 75, 145, **145**
Photo cubes 69, **69**
Photo editing
    careers 57
    color correction **56**, 56–57, **57**
    photo correction **54**, 54–55, **55**
    to tell a story **52**, 52–53, **53**
Photobombing 65
Photojournalism 10
Pinhole cameras 17, **17**
Pixels 22–23, 153
Point-and-shoot cameras **24**, 24–25,
    79
Point of view **128**, 128–129, **129**, 153
Polaroid cameras 11
Porta, Giambattista della 10
Portrait photography see People,
    photography of
Prints 63, **63**, 68, **68**

R

Raw file format 61, 153
Red-eye syndrome 25, **25**, 96, **96**
Reed, Jim 142–143
Resolution 22, **22**, 153
Reza 123, **123**
Rotate 54
Rule of thirds **118**, 118–119, **119**, 153

S

Sartore, Joel **102**, 102–103
Sasson, Steven 11
Saturation 56
Scrapbooks 68, **68**
Selfies 64, 65, **65**
Sensors 21, **21**, 153
Sepia-toned images 26, **27**
Seurat, Georges 110
Shadows **90**, 90–91, **91**, 126
Sharing photos 64, **64**, 66, **66–67**
Sharpen 55
Shiras, George 134
Shutter 16, **16**, 153
Shutter button 16, **16**, 153
Shutter speed 76–77, **80**, 80–81,
    81, 150
Side lighting 89, **89**
Smartphones **26**, 26–27, 75, 145, **145**
Smile-detection app 75
Social media 64, **64**
Soft light 82, **82**
Sports photography 18, **18**, 58–59,
    58–59, 150
Storing your photos **62**, 62–63, **63**
Storyboards 33

Street photography **28**, 28–29, **29**,
    137, **137**
Subject
    closer shots 112, **112**
    definition 108, **108**, 108–109,
    109, 153
    make it rule **130–149**
Sunprints 37, **37**
Szathmari, Carol 10

T

Telephoto lenses
    compressing patterns 127
    definition 153
    depth of field 77, 78
    fashion photography 51
    focal length 18, 19
    uses 18
Telescopes 19, **19**
Textures 124, **124**
Thiessen, Mark 89, **89**
Thompson, William 31
3-D images
    human eye vs. camera eye **72**,
    72–73, **73**
    make a 3-D illusion 73, **73**
    paintings 83, **83**
    shading 90, **90**
TIFF 61, 153
Time exposures 84, **92**, 92–93, **93**
Timeline 10–11, **10–11**
Tint 56
Top lighting 88, **88**
Toy cameras 38, **38**
Travel photography **146–149**
Tripods 45, **45**, 48, **48**, 153, 154
Tungsten 84
Twilight **84**, 84–85, **85**

U

Underwater cameras **30**, 30–31,
    31, 154

V

Vermeer, Johannes 10
Vertical shots **120**, 120–121, **121**
Video cameras 11, **11**, 32, **32**
Viewfinder 16, **16**, 46, 153

W

Weather photography 142–143,
    142–143
Westergren, Dan 39, **39**
Whistler, James McNeill 110
White balance 95, **95**, 150, 153
Wide-angle lenses 18, 77, 78, 153
Wildlife photography 18, **18**, **132–135**
Winer, Jed 67, **67**

Z

Zahl, Paul 113
Zoom lenses 21, **21**, 25, 49, 112, 153

CREDiTS AND ACKNOWLEDGMENTS

NGK PHOTO GUIDE PHOTO CREDITS

GI: Getty Images   IS: iStockphoto   NGC: National Geographic Creative   SS: Shutterstock

FRONT COVER (BACKGROUND/INSIDE PHONE), John Giustina/GI; (INSET-UPLE), Dimitri Otis/GI; (INSET-CTR LE), Katherine Feng/Minden Pictures; (INSET-LOLE), Zeynep Thomas/GI; (INSET-LORT), cunaplus/SS **BACK COVER** (UP), Eric Kruszewski/NGC; (CTR), wavebreakmedia/SS **SPINE** travnikovstudio/IS **FRONT MATTER** 1, holbox/SS; 2–3, travnikovstudio/IS; 4, wavebreakmedia/SS; 5 (UPLE), volleyballgirl1/NG KIDS My Shot; 5 (UPRT), Bert Folsom/Alamy; 5 (LOLE), Annie Griffiths; 5 (LORT), theowl/NG KIDS My Shot; 6–7 (BACKGROUND), Annie Griffiths; 6, Mark Thiessen/NGS; 7 (A), Annie Griffiths; 7 (B), S.Borisov/SS; 7 (D), fortheloveofadog/NG KIDS My Shot; 7 (C), Annie Griffiths; 8, NGS; 9 (A), Sergey Dubrov/SS; 9 (B), Rich Carey/SS; 9 (C), David Doubilet/NGC; 9 (D), David Doubilet /NGC; 9 (E), Paul Street/Alamy; 9 (F), Brian J. Skerry/NGC; 9 (I), Christian Carollo/SS; 9 (J), Noradoa/SS; 9 (K), Mark Thiessen/NGC; 9 (L), bunghiuz eduard mihai/SS; 9 (M), Annie Griffiths; 10 (A), Mario Carlini/Iguana Press/GI; 10 (B), Oxford Science Archive/Print Collector/GI; 10 (C), Corbis; 10 (D), Roger Fenton/Corbis; 11 (A), Eadweard Muybridge/Corbis; 11 (B), Bettmann/Corbis; 11 (C), Bettmann/Corbis; 11 (D), SimonGaberscik/IS; 11 (E), Jules Gervais Courtellemont/NGC; 11 (F), AP Images/David Duprey; 11 (G), rmnoa357/SS; 12 (BOTH), Annie Griffiths; 13 (ALL), Annie Griffiths **EQUIPMENT BASICS** 14–15, Milkovasa/SS; 16 (UP), Slim Films; 16 (CTR), Rebecca Hale/NGS; 16 (LO), Fouad A. Saad/SS; 17 (UP), Abelardo Morell/NGC; 17 (RT), Stuart Armstrong; 18 (A), JaysonPhotography/SS; 18 (B), Neil Johnson/NGS; 18 (C), Stefan Holm/SS; 18 (D–G), Neil Johnson/NGS; 18 (H), Svetlana Yudina/SS; 18 (I), Neil Johnson/NGS; 19 (ALL), Stuart Armstrong; 20 (UP), Aleksandar Mijatovic/SS; 20 (LOLE), scanrail/IS; 20 (INSET), jocic/SS; 20 (LE CTR), bogdan ionescu/SS; 20 (INSET - UPRT), Dimitri Otis/GI; 20–21 (LE), Oleksiy Mark/SS;21 (UPRT), TungCheung/SS; 21 (LORT), B Calkins/SS; 22 (UP), Emilymilly/NG KIDS My Shot; 22 (LOLE/LORT), estima/IS; 23, Stuart Armstrong; 24 (UP), Rebecca Hale/NGS; 24 (LO), iordani/SS; 25 (UPLE/UPRT/CTR LE/CTR RT), Tzubasa/SS; 25 (LOLE/LORT), Frans Lanting/NGC; 26 (UP), Warren Goldswain/SS; 26 (LOLE/LORT), Rebecca Hale/NGS; 27 (UP), Philippe Kahn; 27 (CTR), DreamInColour/NG KIDS My Shot; 27 (LOLE/LO CTR/LORT), Pshenichka/SS; 28, Annie Griffiths; 29 (UPLE/UPRT/CTR LE/CTR RT), Annie Griffiths; 29 (LO), Henri Cartier-Bresson/Magnum Photos; 30 (LE), Sergey Dubrov/SS; 30 (RT), Rich Carey/SS; 31 (UP/CTR), David Doubilet/NGC; 31 (LOLE), Paul Street/Alamy; 31 (LORT), Brian J. Skerry/NGC; 32 (UP), gilotyna4/SS; 32 (CTR LE), lucadp/IS; 32 (CTR RT), marinuse - People/Alamy; 32 (LO), Steve Skjold/Alamy; 33 (UP), NEGOVURA/SS; 33 (CTR), Stuart Armstrong; 33 (LO), Monkey Business Images/SS; 34, Annie Griffiths; 35 (UP), S.Borisov/SS; 35 (CTR), Annie Griffiths; 35 (LO), Fortheloveofadog/NG KIDS My Shot; 36 (UP), showcake/SS; 36 (CTR), chrisdorney/SS; 36 (LOLE), Michael Nichols/NGC; 36 (LORT), Lynn Johnson/NGC; 37 (ALL), Mark Thiessen/NGS; 38 (UP), Action Photos/SS; 38 (LO), 1Photodiva/IS; 39 (UPLE), Daniel R. Westergren; 39 (UPRT), Mark Thiessen/NGS; 39 (CTR), Alex Melnick/SS; 39 (LO), bikeriderlondon/SS; 40 (UP), Pixsooz/SS; 40 (CTR LE), keantian/SS; 40 (CTR CTR), jocic/SS; 40 (CTR RT), neelsky/SS; 40 (CTR), snowblurred/SS; 40 (LO), Iamnao/SS; 40 (LOLE), MJ Prototype/SS; 41 (UPRT), Bert Folsom/Alamy; 41 (UP), NorGal/SS; 41 (CTR), Mike Booth/Alamy; 41 (LOLE), Photomaxx/SS; 41 (LORT), Mark Thiessen/NGS **HOLD IT RIGHT ... AND FOCUS** 42–43, frans lemmens/Alamy; 44 (UP), Trevor kelly/SS; 44 (LOLE), Brooke Whatnall/NGC; 44 (LORT), wavebreakmedia/SS; 45 (UP), Peregrine-Falcon/NG KIDS My Shot; 45 (CTR), GVictoria/SS; 45 (LO), Philippe Henry/Oxford Scientific RM/GI; 46, Zdenek Rosenthaler/SS; 47 (UPLE), TTstudio/SS; 47 (UPLE-INSET-A), photka/SS; 47 (UPLE-INSET-B), Thomas Bethge/SS; 47 (LOLE), TTstudio/SS; 47 (LOLE-INSET-A), photka/SS; 47 (LOLE-INSET-B), Thomas Bethge/SS; 47 (LORT), Michael Nichols/NGC; 48 (UP), Ron Chapple Stock/IS; 48 (LO), Jeff Farmer/IS; 49 (ALL), Mark Thiessen/NGS; 50, Annie Griffiths; 51 (LE), George F. Mobley/NGC; 51 (RT), ByFaith/NG KIDS My Shot; 52–53 (BACKGROUND), Svetl/iStock; 52, Mark Thiessen/NGS; 53 (1), EpicStockMedia/SS; 53 (2), Natursports/SS; 53 (3), Kaori Ando/Image Source/GI; 53 (4), Image Source/GI; 53 (5), Image Source/GI; 54 (BOTH), John Lund/Photographer's Choice RF/GI; 55 (UPLE/UPRT), Phong.Tran/SS; 55 (LOLE/LORT), Hung Chung Chih/SS; 56 (UPLE/UPRT), hammett79/SS; 56 (CTR/LO), Ralph Lee Hopkins/NGC; 57 (UP), Kelley Miller/NGS; 57 (CTR A), Nick Free/iStock; 57 (CTR B), wynnter/istock; 57 (LOLE/LO CTR), Lisa A/SS; 57 (LORT), Hollygraphic/SS; 58 (UP), Annie Griffiths; 58 (LO), mckadenator/NG KIDS My Shot; 59 (UP/CTR), Annie Griffiths; 59 (LOLE), StefanoT/SS; 59 (LORT), TheGuyWithACamera/NG KIDS My Shot; 60 (iPHONE)), Popartic/iStock; 60, Joel Sartore/NGC; 61 (UP-MONITOR), AndSim/iStock; 61 (UP), Paul Nicklen/NGC; 61

Staff for This Book
Erica Green, *Senior Editor*
Jim Hiscott, Jr., *Art Director*
Barbara Brownell Grogan, *Editor/ Project Manager*
Project Design Company, *Designer*
Stuart Armstrong, *Graphics Artist*
Lori Epstein and Kelley Miller, *Senior Photo Editors*
Paige Towler, *Editorial Assistant*
Sanjida Rashid and Rachel Kenny, *Design Production Assistants*
Michael Cassady, *Rights Clearance Specialist*
Grace Hill, *Managing Editor*
Michael O'Connor, *Production Editor*
Lewis R. Bassford, *Production Manager*
George Bounelis, *Manager, Production Services*
Susan Borke, *Legal and Business Affairs*

Published by the National Geographic Society
Gary E. Knell, *President and CEO*
John M. Fahey, *Chairman of the Board*
Melina Gerosa Bellows, *Chief Education Officer*
Declan Moore, *Chief Media Officer*
Hector Sierra, *Senior Vice President and General Manager, Book Division*

Senior Management Team, Kids Publishing and Media Nancy Laties Feresten, *Senior Vice President;* Jennifer Emmett, *Vice President, Editorial Director, Kids Books;* Julie Vosburgh Agnone, *Vice President, Editorial Operations;* Rachel Buchholz, *Editor and Vice President, NG Kids magazine;* Michelle Sullivan, *Vice President, Kids Digital;* Eva Absher-Schantz, *Design Director;* Jay Sumner, *Photo Director;* Hannah August, *Marketing Director;* R. Gary Colbert, *Production Director*

Digital Anne McCormack, *Director;* Laura Goertzel, Sara Zeglin, *Producers;* Emma Rigney, *Creative Producer;* Bianca Bowman, *Assistant Producer;* Natalie Jones, *Senior Product Manager*

The National Geographic Society is one of the world's largest nonprofit scientific and educational organizations. Founded in 1888 to "increase and diffuse geographic knowledge," the Society's mission is to inspire people to care about the planet. It reaches more than 400 million people worldwide each month through its official journal, *National Geographic*, and other magazines; National Geographic Channel; television documentaries; music; radio; films; books; DVDs; maps; exhibitions; live events; school publishing programs; interactive media; and merchandise. National Geographic has funded more than 10,000 scientific research, conservation, and exploration projects and supports an education program promoting geographic literacy.

For more information, please visit nationalgeographic .com, call 1-800-NGS LINE (647-5463), or write to the following address:
National Geographic Society
1145 17th Street N.W.
Washington, D.C. 20036-4688 U.S.A.

Visit us online at nationalgeographic.com/books

For librarians and teachers: ngchildrensbooks.org

More for kids from National Geographic:
kids.nationalgeographic.com

For information about special discounts for bulk purchases, please contact National Geographic Books Special Sales: ngspecsales@ngs.org

For rights or permissions inquiries, please contact National Geographic Books Subsidiary Rights: ngbookrights@ngs.org

Paperback ISBN: 978-1-4263-2066-8
Reinforced library binding ISBN: 978-1-4263-2067-5

Printed in the United States of America
15/QGT-CML/1